101 THINGS HOME OWNERS SHOULD KNOW

Expert Advice for Buying, Maintaining, and Improving Your Home

JACK ROSS

Copyright 2024.

SPOTLIGHT MEDIA

ISBN: 978-1-951806-60-6

For questions, please reach out to:

Support@ActivityWizo.com

All Rights Reserved.

No part of this book may be reproduced or transmitted in any form or by any means, electronic or mechanical, including photocopying, recording, or by any other form without written permission from the publisher.

FREE BOOK

SCAN TO GET OUR NEXT BOOK FOR FREE

TABLE OF CONTENTS

CHAPTER ONE: BUYING YOUR FIRST HOME 1

[1] UNDERSTANDING THE HOME-BUYING PROCESS 2

[2] FINDING THE RIGHT REAL ESTATE AGENT 3

[3] IMPORTANCE OF A HOME INSPECTION 4

[4] UNDERSTANDING MORTGAGE OPTIONS........................5

[5] BUDGETING FOR YOUR NEW HOME 7

[6] NEGOTIATING THE BEST DEAL...8

[7] IMPORTANCE OF LOCATION 9

[8] UNDERSTANDING CLOSING COSTS 10

[9] IMPORTANCE OF A GOOD CREDIT SCORE 11

[10] CHOOSING BETWEEN A NEW OR OLDER HOME........12

CHAPTER TWO: HOME MAINTENANCE BASICS 15

[11] ESSENTIAL TOOLS EACH HOME OWNER SHOULD HAVE..16

[12] CREATING A HOME MAINTENANCE SCHEDULE 17

[13] SEASONAL MAINTENANCE TASKS................................18

[14] HOW TO IDENTIFY AND FIX COMMON ISSUES..........19

[15] MAINTAINING YOUR HVAC SYSTEM.............................21

[16] CLEANING AND MAINTAINING YOUR ROOF 22

[17] CARING FOR HARDWOOD FLOORS..............................23

[18] MAINTAINING WINDOWS 24

CHAPTER THREE: LANDSCAPING AND OUTDOOR CARE . 27

[19] BASIC LAWN CARE AND MAINTENANCE 28

[20] TIPS FOR MAINTAINING OUTDOOR STRUCTURES ... 29

[21] CHOOSING THE RIGHT PLANTS FOR YOUR GARDEN 30

[22] MAINTAINING A GARDEN 32

[23] DIY LANDSCAPING PROJECTS 34

[24] SEASONAL OUTDOOR MAINTENANCE 34

[25] INSTALLING AND MAINTAINING IRRIGATION SYSTEMS 38

[26] PEST CONTROL FOR YOUR YARD 39

[27] MULCHING AND FERTILIZING TIPS 41

[28] CREATING OUTDOOR LIVING SPACES 43

CHAPTER FOUR: HOME SAFETY AND SECURITY 47

[29] SMOKE AND CARBON MONOXIDE DETECTORS 48

[30] TIPS FOR SECURING YOUR HOME 49

[31] CREATING A HOME EMERGENCY PLAN 50

[32] FIRE SAFETY TIPS AND EQUIPMENT 51

[33] CHILDPROOFING YOUR HOME 52

[34] PROTECTING YOUR HOME DURING VACATIONS 53

[35] UNDERSTANDING HOME INSURANCE POLICIES 54

[36] SPECIALIZED HOME INSURANCE 55

[37] EMERGENCY PREPAREDNESS FOR NATURAL DISASTERS 56

[38] KEEPING YOUR HOME WELL LIT 57

CHAPTER FIVE: ENERGY EFFICIENCY AND SUSTAINABILITY 59

[39] TIPS FOR REDUCING ENERGY CONSUMPTION 60

[40] UNDERSTANDING AND IMPROVING HOME INSULATION 61

[41] BENEFITS OF ENERGY-EFFICIENT APPLIANCES 62

[42] DIY PROJECTS TO INCREASE ENERGY EFFICIENCY .. 63

[43] EXPLORING RENEWABLE ENERGY OPTIONS 65

[44] SIMPLE WAYS TO MAKE YOUR HOME MORE ECO-FRIENDLY 66

[45] USING PROGRAMMABLE THERMOSTATS................... 67

[46] SEALING WINDOWS AND DOORS 68

[47] WATER-SAVING TIPS... 68

[48] RECYCLING AND WASTE REDUCTION AT HOME...... 69

CHAPTER SIX: HOME IMPROVEMENT PROJECTS 71

[49] PLANNING AND BUDGETING FOR RENOVATION..... 72

[50] CHOOSING THE RIGHT CONTRACTORS....................... 73

[51] DIY HOME IMPROVEMENT TIPS.................................... 74

[52] COMMON MISTAKES TO AVOID IN-HOME PROJECTS 75

[53] PERMITS AND REGULATIONS FOR HOME RENOVATIONS 77

[54] INCREASING YOUR HOME'S VALUE THROUGH IMPROVEMENTS 78

[55] KITCHEN RENOVATION TIPS 79

[56] BATHROOM REMODELING IDEAS 80

[57] DRIVEWAYS AND WALKWAYS 81

[58] IMPROVING CURB APPEAL 82

CHAPTER SEVEN: INTERIOR DESIGN AND DECORATING . 85

[59] BASIC PRINCIPLES OF INTERIOR DESIGN 86

[60] TIPS FOR CHOOSING PAINT COLORS AND FINISHES 87

[61] DIY DECORATING IDEAS 88

[62] ARRANGING FURNITURE FOR FUNCTIONALITY AND AESTHETICS 89

[63] INCORPORATING PERSONAL STYLE INTO YOUR HOME 90

[64] DECORATING ON A BUDGET 91

[65] CHOOSING WINDOW TREATMENTS 92

[66] CREATING A COHESIVE COLOR SCHEME 93

[67] USING MIRRORS AND LIGHTING EFFECTIVELY 94

[68] SEASONAL DECORATING TIPS 95

CHAPTER EIGHT: PLUMBING AND ELECTRICAL SYSTEMS 97

[69] BASIC PLUMBING REPAIRS 98

[70] UNDERSTANDING YOUR HOME'S PLUMBING SYSTEM 98

[71] COMMON PLUMBING PROBLEMS AND FIXES 99

[72] ELECTRICAL SAFETY 100

[73] REPLACING A WALL OUTLET 101

[74] INSTALLING NEW FIXTURES 102

[75] WHEN TO CALL A PROFESSIONAL 103

[76] TIPS FOR MAINTAINING YOUR HOME'S SYSTEMS .. 103

[77] UNDERSTANDING YOUR WATER HEATER 104

[78] DEALING WITH LOW WATER PRESSURE 105

[79] ELECTRICAL PANEL BASICS 106

CHAPTER NINE: HOME OWNERSHIP FINANCIAL TIPS 109

[80] UNDERSTANDING PROPERTY TAXES 110

[81] TIPS FOR BUDGETING AND SAVING AS A HOME OWNER 110

[82] MANAGING HOME-RELATED EXPENSES 111

[83] UNDERSTANDING HOME EQUITY 111

[84] REFINANCING 112

[85] PLANNING FOR FUTURE HOME EXPENSES 112

[86] IMPORTANCE OF AN EMERGENCY FUND 113

[87] TAX BENEFITS OF HOME OWNERSHIP 114

[88] PAYING OFF YOUR MORTGAGE EARLY 115

[89] OVERALL FINANCIAL HEALTH 115

CHAPTER TEN: HOME CLEANING AND ORGANIZATION 117

[90] CREATING A CLEANING SCHEDULE 118

[91] TIPS FOR DEEP CLEANING YOUR HOME 119

[92] ORGANIZING YOUR HOME ROOM BY ROOM 120

[93] DECLUTTERING TIPS AND TRICKS 121

[94] USING PROFESSIONAL CLEANING SERVICES 123

[95] GREEN CLEANING SOLUTIONS 124

[96] DIY CLEANING SOLUTIONS 125

[97] STORING SEASONAL ITEMS 126

[98] ORGANIZING YOUR GARAGE AND BASEMENT 127

[99] EFFECTIVE USE OF STORAGE CONTAINERS 128

CHAPTER ELEVEN: PREPARING FOR THE FUTURE 131

[100] PLANNING FOR POTENTIAL MARKET CHANGES. 132

[101] PREPARING FOR RETIREMENT 133

AFTERWARD 135

CHAPTER ONE:
BUYING YOUR FIRST HOME

[1] UNDERSTANDING THE HOME-BUYING PROCESS

Buying a new home is an exciting and often nerve-wracking process. Whether it's your first time buying a home, or you've done it before, the process can be complicated. It involves numerous steps and documents, all of which have a specific role to play at a particular time.

It's important to surround yourself with experts you can trust during the process of finding and purchasing a home. Since regulations and the market change over time, you should solicit the advice of experts even if you've bought and sold homes before. Real estate agents can help with everything from finding your home to making a successful offer. In addition to your real estate agent, you'll most likely need support from a lawyer, a representative at a financial institution, and a home inspector.

The home-buying process begins with establishing your financial health. When you're ready, you'll hire a real estate agent, establish a budget for your new home, and ideally seek preapproval from a reputable lending institution. Armed with your preapproval, you can begin shopping for new homes.

This usually involves a great deal of online research as well as frequent visits to open houses. When you find the right home for you, you and your realtor will put together a formal offer on the home that aims to fit your budget and meet the expectations of the sellers. If your offer is accepted, you'll confirm the details of the sale with the sellers, obtain your official mortgage approval, and complete a home inspection. If all goes smoothly, you'll move ahead toward closing and making the sale official.

This book provides a general overview of what to expect from a successful home search. However, each step of the process brings its own tasks and potential challenges, which your real estate agent will be well positioned to guide you through.

[2] FINDING THE RIGHT REAL ESTATE AGENT

Your realtor's job is to advise you as you search for a new home. While you bear the responsibility for being well informed about the process, the realtor is there to provide guidance on all the small details that you may not reasonably be able to learn on your own. You will inevitably place a lot of trust and responsibility in your real estate agent, so it's worth taking the time to choose a realtor carefully. Like any major purchase or investment, you should research your options in depth.

Talk with friends and family to get their recommendations for reputable real estate agents in your area. Many home-buying apps also recommend local realtors, and you can research top real estate agents in your area. Once you've identified a few real estate agents or realty companies that look promising, reach out to them to request introductory meetings.

It's a good idea to speak with a few different agents before committing to one so that you can ensure your communication styles and expectations for the process align. Ask detailed questions during these introductory meetings and get the details in writing.

[3]
IMPORTANCE OF A HOME INSPECTION

The home inspection is an important step in the process of buying a home. Home inspections exist specifically to protect and inform the homebuyer. It's extremely risky to purchase a home without completing a home inspection first.

The home inspection typically takes place after your offer has been accepted by the sellers but before the date of closing. During a home inspection, you will accompany the inspector as they walk around the home's interior and exterior, examining the home's features. Home inspections are prescribed procedures, which means that the inspector will be working from a standardized list of items and features to examine.

A few of the major things that an inspector will examine include the walls, roof, attic or basement, and foundation. It also includes an examination of heating and air conditioning systems, plumbing, and electrical systems. It's important to note that the inspector will only evaluate the elements of the home that are readily accessible. This means that the inspector will not evaluate any element of the home that's enclosed by walls.

Upon completion of the home inspection—which will likely take several hours—you will receive a detailed report of the findings from the home inspector. The report will include the condition of every element in the home they examined. Based on this report, you may feel confident moving forward with the purchase of your home. Alternatively, you may find that you want to renegotiate some terms with the seller, particularly if the home inspection turns up any issues that will be time-consuming or very costly to repair.

[4]
UNDERSTANDING MORTGAGE OPTIONS

Most homebuyers make use of a mortgage to purchase their home. A mortgage is a loan from a bank or financial institution. The financial institution lends you money upfront so that you can purchase your home. You're expected to pay back that full loan over time through regular monthly payments plus interest.

There are many different types of mortgages, and you'll need to research your options before committing to one. You can also meet with representatives of different financial institutions to determine which mortgage product is best suited to your needs. The most common mortgage types are 15-year and 30-year fixed-rate mortgages. These mortgages will take either 15 or 30 years to pay off, respectively, for a person making full, on-time monthly payments.

The fixed-rate part refers to the interest rate on the loan. A fixed-rate mortgage guarantees that your interest rate will stay the same over the full life of the mortgage. So, if you can secure a mortgage with a low interest rate, having a fixed-rate mortgage is good news. This means that the rate will never increase for your mortgage, regardless of the fluctuations of interest rates elsewhere in the market.

In contrast, an adjustable-rate mortgage means that the interest rate stays the same for a set amount of time, but then can change periodically to reflect various interest rates. Adjustable-rate mortgages may be attractive for buyers who are purchasing their home at a time of especially high interest rates. In that scenario, the possibility that the interest rate on the mortgage will decrease over time is beneficial. Always read the fine print in the mortgage terms to make sure you fully understand when and how much the interest is permitted to change over time.

Certain buyers may benefit from special mortgage products that target specific populations or situations. For example, the U.S. Department of Veterans Affairs supports mortgages with special terms for veterans. Other government offices, including the Federal Housing Administration and the Department of Agriculture, offer special mortgage options to support low-income or first-time homebuyers, farm owners, and other groups. If you have reason to believe that you may qualify for one of these special loan programs, they are worth researching in further detail.

[5]
BUDGETING FOR YOUR NEW HOME

For most people, a home is the single largest purchase they will make in their lifetime. Therefore, it's not surprising that it tends to require long-term planning, saving, and budgeting. While most people purchase a home primarily with the help of a mortgage loan, most homebuyers are also required to put down some money in a lump sum.

The sum of money that is paid upfront during the home buying process is called the down payment, which is a percentage of the total home purchase price. It typically ranges between 5 percent and 20 percent of the total price. For example, if you're hoping to purchase a home that costs around $250,000, then you should be prepared to pay up to $50,000 at the time of closing. In addition to the down payment, you will likely face additional costs at the time of closing, which include realtor and appraisal fees, taxes, and more.

Beyond budgeting for the down payment, take a moment to consider your current income and expenses. How much can you afford to pay monthly as a mortgage payment in addition to the utilities and general maintenance that come with home ownership? Be honest with yourself about the numbers that will be manageable for you. Understanding the realities of your monthly budget will allow you to work with a financial professional to determine the mortgage amount—and the home purchase price amount—that makes sense for you.

[6]
NEGOTIATING THE BEST DEAL

Buying a home is a process that requires a great deal of negotiation, typically beyond just the price of the house. You can also negotiate the closing date, home repairs, and more. Your real estate agent will be a good resource and advocate for you throughout these negotiations.

When you are ready to make an offer on a home, you can work with your real estate agent to determine a strategic offer price. Your goal is to offer a purchase price that works within your budget but is also competitive relative to other offers the seller might receive. When determining what to offer, consider the list price of the home. You can offer the exact amount, or you can decide to go higher or lower.

For example, if the house you're looking at needs repairs and has been listed for a long time without any offers, you may be able to offer below the listing price and still be competitive. On the other hand, if a house is priced competitively already and you know it has interest from other buyers, you may need to name a higher amount to make your offer stand out.

When you make your offer, the seller may either reject it outright, accept it, or come back with a counteroffer. If you enter a negotiation on the purchase price, it's important to understand the seller's priorities and what it will take for them to move forward. You're not required to meet their desired terms, but understanding their goals will help you determine whether it's a path that's worth pursuing.

[7]
IMPORTANCE OF LOCATION

It's an old adage in the real estate business: location, location, location! A home's location is widely considered to be one of its most important, if not its single most important, attribute. This is because most elements of a home can be changed, but the location is permanent.

If the house's fixtures or features are outdated or broken, you can conceivably have those replaced. In fact, an entire home can be torn down and a new one built in its place to reflect a home owner's exact personal preferences. However, you can't change the immediate surroundings or move a house to another city.

Location matters a great deal when it comes to the listing price due to differences in the cost of living. Homes that are in "prime" locations—whether due to their convenience, natural beauty, privacy, or some other factor—typically sell for more than their counterparts in less desirable locations.

Once you've identified your priorities regarding a home's location, consider how much you're willing to pay. Keep in mind that location is a factor that may be worth paying more for, especially if you also need to weigh factors like school districts.

[8]
UNDERSTANDING CLOSING COSTS

Closing costs are the fees that you will need to pay at the time of purchasing your home. Since closing costs are calculated separately from, and in addition to, your down payment on the home, you must budget for them accordingly.

Typically, closing costs represent between 2 percent and 5 percent of the total mortgage amount. They consist of fees for the loan application, underwriting, title insurance, and attorney. You'll also be responsible for paying any real estate commissions at closing.

In the days and weeks leading up to your closing date, you will receive documentation from your lending institution that specifies the precise amount of your closing costs so that you can be sure to have that money ready on closing day. It typically must be paid in the form of a certified check or wire transfer.

[9]
IMPORTANCE OF A GOOD CREDIT SCORE

Your credit score is an indication of your past credit behavior. It serves as a general indicator of how likely a particular individual is to pay back their loans on time. Credit scores range from 300 (poor) to 850 (excellent), and your score is taken into consideration whenever you apply for a loan.

When applying for a mortgage, your credit score will partially determine who is willing to lend you money, what loan products are available to you, and the interest rates you will receive. For these reasons, having a healthy credit score of 670 or above is vital. You can find your credit score from most credit card companies, banks, or other lenders where you currently have accounts open.

Alternatively, you can obtain a free credit report from a nonprofit credit counselor or housing counselor. These professionals are trained by the Department of Housing and Urban Development, and you can find lists of their contact information online. Finally, many paid services will provide you with a credit report for a fee. Be sure to explore the free options described above before paying one of these companies for your credit report.

If you find that you need to improve your credit score to qualify for more favorable mortgage terms, this process is fairly straightforward. The essential way to improve your credit score is to make on-time payments for all debt you currently hold. As you continuously demonstrate a pattern of on-time payments, your credit score will gradually increase.

Paying off existing loans can help raise your score significantly, so prioritize paying down your debt before buying a new home. While you're working to improve your credit score, try to avoid applying for any new loans or credit cards. Simply applying for new lines of credit can harm your current credit score.

[10]
CHOOSING BETWEEN A NEW OR OLDER HOME

The process of choosing a home requires a careful understanding of both your needs and your wants. Most people can conjure a long list of features they would love to have in their dream home, but most of those are purely wants. Consider your lifestyle, finances, the amount of time you have available, and how you like to spend that time; all these factors can help you decide on the characteristics that are most important for you.

While there are many factors that can be used to differentiate between homes on the market, one of the most basic factors is the age of the home. The terms new and older are subjective and will mean different things to different people. For some people, a new home is one built in the last year or two, while an older home was built 20 years ago. For others, particularly in different parts of the world, an old home may be 100 years old or more, making that 20-year-old house "new" by comparison.

Generally speaking, an older home may require more frequent and extensive maintenance than one that's newer. While this isn't always the case, you should be prepared for ongoing maintenance and upgrades in homes that are over 20 years old. For some home owners, this is actually a benefit. If you are handy and enjoy working around the home in your spare time, then having projects to tinker with on the weekends may be a perfect fit for you. Older homes also typically sell at lower prices than newer ones, making these homes desirable for those with limited budgets.

In contrast, those who lack the skill or the time to conduct their own home repairs may find that an older home isn't the best choice for them. It will be very costly to hire a professional for each project around the home. A newer home is less likely to need significant renovations or major repairs. Consider these factors as you think through the age and aesthetic of the home that will best fit your needs and suit your tastes.

CHAPTER TWO: HOME MAINTENANCE BASICS

[11]
ESSENTIAL TOOLS EACH HOME OWNER SHOULD HAVE

There are certain tasks around the home that the average person has the skills to complete. Being able to take care of some minor repairs can not only instill a feeling of confidence, but it can also help save money in the long run.

Even home owners who aren't handy or who don't plan to take on any major home repair or renovation projects will need to invest in some basic tools and equipment. Some of these are products you will need to maintain a clean home, such as a vacuum cleaner, a plunger, and a mop. If your home has a patio, balcony, or yard, you may also need a rake, spade, or snow shovel.

Beyond the cleanliness of the home, every home owner will find that they need to take care of projects around the house at some point. While you can call in a professional for large projects, you should have utility scissors, a hammer, screwdrivers, a measuring tape, a level, and paintbrushes on hand for small tasks. Pliers and a wrench set will also come in handy, and you may find yourself in need of a basic stud finder if you plan to hang anything heavy on your walls.

Don't forget to keep a small supply of flashlights and candles somewhere easily accessible in your home. In the case of a power outage, you will need to be able to locate these quickly.

Additionally, ensure that you always have a stock of batteries available for emergencies.

[12]
CREATING A HOME MAINTENANCE SCHEDULE

There are many ongoing, routine tasks that are involved in maintaining a safe, functional, and tidy home. These tasks vary by home. Some of these tasks you can do on your own, while others may require the help of trained professionals.

To stay on top of home maintenance, many home owners follow a general schedule. It's logical to divide the schedule by season since so many home maintenance tasks are tied to a particular time of year. As you consider the items that should appear on your home maintenance checklist, remember to consider both indoor and outdoor features of your home.

The following are the indoor features of the home that should appear on your regular maintenance schedule: changing HVAC filters, cleaning fireplaces and chimneys, and deep cleaning floors and walls. You should also periodically clean carpets, drains, grout, dishwasher filters, curtains, and dryer vents.

The following are outdoor features of a home that should not be overlooked during yearly maintenance schedules: grass seeding, yard debris removal, snow removal, gutter maintenance, and landscaping.

[13]
SEASONAL MAINTENANCE TASKS

While the exact items on your maintenance schedule will depend on the details of your home, below are some ideas for common maintenance tasks in each season.

Spring

- Check the roof for any damage that may have occurred in the winter.
- Clean up sticks and other debris that may have accumulated in the yard or gutters.
- Tidy and mulch garden beds.
- Seed your lawn.
- Clean the exterior of all windows.

Summer

- Hire a professional to start up your irrigation systems.
- Inspect the home's foundation for any holes where pests can enter.
- Have your chimney cleaned and inspected before the cold weather begins.

Fall

- Rake and clean up yard debris.
- Hire a professional to turn off any existing irrigation system.
- Check the sealing around your home's windows to make sure they're in good condition.

Winter

- Check for icicles and ice dams to prevent damage to your roof.
- Cover your air conditioning unit.
- Move patio furniture into storage.

[14]
HOW TO IDENTIFY AND FIX COMMON ISSUES

Mold

Mold has potentially serious health consequences. If you have a mold issue in your home, you will likely identify it either by seeing or smelling it. Mold appears fuzzy or slimy and will be discolored compared to its surrounding materials. It often releases a musty, unpleasant odor. Mold grows fastest in areas that are relatively dark and damp, so you should pay special attention while cleaning kitchens and bathrooms.

If you do find mold in your home, you will need to remedy the problem immediately. This means not only removing the existing mold but also taking steps to ensure mold won't grow again in the same location. If the mold growth you found covers an area of more than a few square feet, it's best to bring in a professional to address the problem. However, if you find a small mold growth, you can likely handle it yourself.

If you find mold on a soft or porous material (e.g., insulation), then the affected material will need to be removed from the home and discarded. It's not possible to fully remove mold from a porous surface. However, if the mold has appeared on a hard, nonporous surface like a pipe, then you can likely clean it. Do so with soap and water and be sure to wear a mask and rubber gloves.

Once the mold has been removed, identify the water source that allowed mold to grow in that area. Take the necessary steps to ensure the area remains clean and dry with adequate airflow in the future.

Pests

You'll likely identify pest infestations either through sight or smell, but you may be able to hear critters moving around. Pest infestations can include things like bed bugs or ants or larger animals like mice and squirrels. These animals will most likely take refuge in your basement, walls, or attic, especially in cold weather.

The best way to handle a pest infestation depends on the type of pest you've encountered. For all pests, one important step is to locate the entry point to your home. Is there a window with a hole in the screen through which insects can enter? Are there holes or cracks in your siding, roof, or foundation? Be sure to identify entry points and seal them off if possible.

Once you've sealed your home and removed any possible food sources to the best of your ability, there are several types of traps available to handle pests of all sizes. If you opt to put out traps for pests, be sure they are placed in areas where children and pets can't access them, especially for traps that contain toxic chemicals.

If you're facing a very significant infestation, or if the pests are likely to cause damage to your home (such as carpenter ants or signs of mice around your wiring), it's best to call in the support of a professional pest removal service.

[15]
MAINTAINING YOUR HVAC SYSTEM

Heating, ventilation, and air conditioning (HVAC) refers to all the parts and systems that work to maintain good air quality and keep your home at a comfortable temperature. Depending on the style of your home, an HVAC system often includes the following:

- Air conditioning units, such as central air conditioning or a mini-split system
- Furnace, boiler, or heat pump
- Thermostat
- Radiators

- Built-in humidifiers or dehumidifiers
- Air filters

HVAC repairs typically require the assistance of an HVAC professional. As a home owner, your responsibility is to provide ongoing preventive maintenance to keep your HVAC system in good working order. This routine preventive maintenance includes replacing air filters throughout your home every 30 to 90 days, cleaning and trimming back vegetation around outdoor HVAC units, and keeping all air registers open so that your system can work properly. In addition to regular maintenance, you should schedule a maintenance check with a professional once per year.

If you ever notice unusual or excessive noise coming from any element of your HVAC system, call in a professional for a consultation. Other reasons to call a professional may include mysteriously rising energy costs. This might indicate that your system is working harder than it should and is due for repairs. You should also call in a professional if you note that any element of your HVAC system doesn't seem to be working effectively.

[16]
CLEANING AND MAINTAINING YOUR ROOF

To maximize its lifespan and efficacy, you should regularly inspect and maintain your roof. If your home has an attic, check it regularly for any wet spots that might indicate a leak in the roof. Make a point to visually inspect your roof from the ground regularly, looking out for any loose or missing shingles or other visible signs of wear and tear.

In addition to watching for any noticeable changes to the roof, home owners should perform some simple, routine maintenance tasks in the spring and fall. Cleaning gutters and trimming back any branches that hang over the roof will help protect and ensure the longevity of your roof.

Most roofs will build up some moss or mildew over time, and this should be cleaned off when it appears. Moss can cause shingles to curl and deform, which makes them more likely to come loose from the roof. While it's possible to perform roof cleaning on your own, most roof-related tasks are best undertaken by professionals due to safety issues.

[17]
CARING FOR HARDWOOD FLOORS

It's a good idea to clean hardwood floors daily to keep dust and dirt from accumulating. Even very small bits of dust and dirt can contribute to scratching and build-up on hardwood floors. In addition to dust removal, hardwood floors should be cleaned with a mop every week. Harsh cleaners can strip the finish from a hardwood floor, so use a cleaning product that's specially formulated to clean wood.

Every few months, it's also necessary to polish hardwood floors with a water-based polish. Polishing regularly helps to maintain your floor's finish, which can otherwise be stripped away over time through use and regular cleaning.

If you maintain daily dust removal, weekly cleaning, and quarterly polishing routines, your hardwood floors should maintain their good condition for several years. On average, hardwood floors need refinishing every 7 to 10 years, so it's important to include that as part of your long-term maintenance plan.

[18] MAINTAINING WINDOWS

The windows throughout your home require both routine and more intensive maintenance to remain functional. Windows allow light and fresh air to circulate throughout your home. On their own, they can contribute significantly to your décor and the feel of a room or space. Some windows are highly decorative themselves, with unique shapes, pane structures, or even colored glass, to draw the eye and give a room a special touch.

More important than the aesthetic is the utility of windows. They regulate the entrance of light and outside air into your home, making them an important part of your home's structure. Faulty windows can create several safety hazards. For example, if the window doesn't latch properly, you might fall through or give an intruder the perfect entrance.

The most basic step to maintaining windows is to keep them clean. This means cleaning each window's interior and exterior glass regularly, as well as wiping down the window frame and sill. While you perform this routine task, you can also use the opportunity to check the window and all its elements for any sign of damage.

Pay special attention to caulking and weather stripping around the window and note any signs of wear and tear. While cleaning, especially on breezy or cold days, check to see if you can feel air flowing around the window. That may be a sign that the seal needs to be reinforced.

A general guideline is to clean window glass twice per year and wipe down internal sills at least once per month. Check for signs of damage or faulty seals during that cleaning. Windows should be re-caulked every five to seven years or whenever there are signs of damage.

CHAPTER THREE: LANDSCAPING AND OUTDOOR CARE

[19]
BASIC LAWN CARE AND MAINTENANCE

Whether you have a small patch of green or an expansive lawn, you'll need to dedicate some time to caring for grass. Except for the winter months in some climates, grass needs care at least twice per month to keep it healthy.

The most familiar task associated with lawn maintenance is mowing. Mowing grass is important not only for aesthetic appeal but also because grass that is allowed to grow too tall can become overrun with ticks and other pests.

The frequency of mowing, as well as the length to which you mow your lawn, will depend both on personal preference and your regional climate. If you live in an arid climate or are enduring a particularly dry stretch, cutting your grass too short could pose a fire hazard. On the other hand, grass grows very quickly when water is plentiful. If you have a rainy spring, you may find that you need to cut your grass more often to prevent it from becoming overgrown.

If you find that your lawn dries out quickly, despite your best efforts to keep it properly mowed and hydrated, then you may want to consider gradually replacing your existing grass with plants that better fit your local climate. There are many different types of grass, so you can try seeding with a type of grass that fits your climate. Some home owners even prefer to seed their lawns with clover or wildflowers because they're typically hardier and attractive to pollinators.

You may also occasionally want to reseed, or over-seed, your lawn to keep it full. Seeding is typically done in the late spring or early fall to avoid the weather being too hot. You can purchase grass seed at most hardware stores. It's important to spread the seed at the density indicated on the packaging. Spreading the seeds too close together or too sparsely can result in unhealthy or irregular grass. While it is possible to spread by hand in small areas, you will probably want to use a simple spreader with wheels for larger areas.

[20]
TIPS FOR MAINTAINING OUTDOOR STRUCTURES

Your property may contain other structures besides your home. These may include fences, decks, porches, sheds, patios, and more. Each of these structures must be carefully maintained to ensure its lasting utility and safety.

These structures should be thoroughly cleaned annually and lightly cleaned and inspected for damage regularly throughout the year. Each of the features described above could be vulnerable to mildew, structural damage, pest infestations, and other issues. During your regular inspections of these structures, be on the lookout for any visible wear and tear, discoloration, rust, and signs of water where you would reasonably expect it to be dry.

Structures made of wood on your property, such as wooden decks and fences, can be lightly cleaned as needed. They should also be resealed and stained or painted on a regular schedule to maintain their durability over time. Patios and porches should be cared for the same way and washed with a power washer, depending on the structure's material.

An outdoor shed must be maintained the same way you maintain your home, just on a smaller scale. This means checking the siding and roof for any damage, cleaning debris off the roof, and resealing the windows regularly.

Many of the maintenance and repairs involved with these types of structures are fairly minor and can probably be done on your own or with the help of a handy friend. However, if you find that a structure is creating a safety risk or needs to be replaced entirely, it's a good idea to get a professional consultation.

[21]
CHOOSING THE RIGHT PLANTS FOR YOUR GARDEN

When choosing the types of plants for your garden, there are a few important considerations to keep in mind. The first decision is whether you want to plant a vegetable or flower garden (or both). If you simply want to enjoy a nice view from afar, then planting flowers is probably best. If the view is less important to you, but you would like to have a practical purpose for what you grow, then you may prefer starting with vegetables.

Keep in mind that different types of plants have different needs for their soil, amount of water, and sunlight throughout the day. If you select the wrong type of plant for your location, you will be disappointed in its performance. Before purchasing seeds or plants, spend a few days watching the location where you want to put your plants. Make a mental note of how the sun hits that spot at different types of day; this information will help you to choose the right type of plant to buy.

For example, if you hope to keep potted plants on your balcony, which is fully shaded all morning but then in full sun until sunset, then you should look for plants that enjoy the afternoon sun. Armed with knowledge about sun exposure, you can try out some plants in your garden. When choosing plants, pay attention not only to how the plants look when you're buying them but also to the expected full size.

If you hope to place plants near each other in the garden, you may not want them to grow to be exactly the same size. Instead, gardeners often look for some short plants to go in the front, medium-height plants to go behind those, and tall plants for the very back. These are known as spillers (the short ones that may hang down the front of a pot), fillers (the middle ones), and thrillers (the tallest ones in the back). Play around with color combinations and have fun creating a combination that suits your tastes.

[22]
MAINTAINING A GARDEN

For gardens to grow, you need to ensure your plants have healthy soil, adequate water, and a lack of pests. If your plants are not growing well, you may find that you need to add fertilizer to the soil. This can give them the added nutrients they are missing, or it can correct a pH imbalance that is impeding growth. Talk with an expert at your local garden center. They will be familiar with common soil issues in your area and may be able to recommend the appropriate treatment to get your plants back on the road to health.

If you have a raised bed or container garden, you will likely purchase the soil that is used for your plants. This will provide you with more control over the growing medium, and you'll also be ensuring that the soil is balanced for your plants' needs. Both vegetables and flowers may benefit from fertilizer throughout the year.

When choosing a fertilizing product, consider the importance of natural versus chemical ingredients. Before spreading any chemical on fruits or vegetables that you plan to eat, make sure the material is intended for edible plants. Using a fertilizer that isn't intended for edible plants may leave toxic materials behind in your fruits and vegetables.

Even a very well-tended garden can be bothered by pests such as slugs, aphids, mites, and beetles that like to munch on plants. When observing your garden, be on the lookout for small black or white spots on stems and leaves, any areas that appear to have been bitten, or conspicuous holes in the leaves of your plants. It's also a good idea to occasionally flip leaves over to look at their undersides, as some bugs like to hang out there.

If you do find that your garden has been invaded by these types of pests, you may need to apply a treatment to the soil or directly to the plants to deter these intruders. Natural products like neem oil offer a chemical-free solution that can be applied directly to plants, or you may opt for a more powerful insecticide. Again, use caution when dealing with edible plants.

Finally, the main task that occupies home gardeners is weeding. Weeding is a simple task that requires only a pair of garden gloves and a few minutes each day. If you pull weeds from your garden for 10 minutes each morning or spend a few minutes after dinner, you can keep the weeds under control while adding a calming ritual to your days.

Some gardeners lack the time to weed daily and instead do all their weeding at once, usually on the weekends. This approach is also fine as long as you protect that weekend weeding time. Weeds can get out of control within a couple of weeks if they aren't regularly pulled up.

[23]
DIY LANDSCAPING PROJECTS

Home owners can take on landscaping projects with as much or as little professional assistance as they desire. It's often possible to landscape entirely on your own if you have the time and strength for the task.

Alternatively, some home owners outsource their landscape design projects entirely to professionals. Some garden centers will provide design services for a small fee, helping you to map out and plan your intended project. They may even suggest what plants or materials to use throughout.

This option allows you to get some expert input on design and the landscaping process but leaves you to do the heavy lifting on your own. This can be a good approach for home owners with a limited budget but ambitious landscape ideas.

[24]
SEASONAL OUTDOOR MAINTENANCE

You're already aware that certain tasks must be performed regularly each year. For example, it's important to rake leaves in the fall. Two of the predictable yearly tasks for many home owners are worthy of further discussion: summer prep and snow removal. This isn't necessarily because these tasks are more complicated or expensive than others but because of the damage or discomfort that can result from a failure to attend to them.

Summer Prep

Winter cleanup, or summer prep, applies to almost every home owner. The exception is if you're in a climate that maintains a consistent temperature and level of moisture throughout the entire calendar year, such as in much of Hawaii and some parts of the southwestern United States. However, most areas see some predictable fluctuation in temperature and/or precipitation throughout the year. For these home owners, it's necessary to attend to maintenance tasks at the end of the cold season to prepare your home for drier, hotter conditions.

Consider the weather conditions in your area and how you will effectively manage your home's indoor climate when the outdoor temperature climbs. If the summer is fairly mild, you may need only well-functioning windows and fans to keep your home comfortable. However, if you face extremely hot or humid summer months, then air-conditioning systems may be needed. Excessive moisture throughout the home due to humidity can cause damage or mold.

Air conditioners are available that serve either as humidifiers or dehumidifiers, depending on the climate, while simultaneously cooling the air in the home. You may choose a simple window unit, a permanently installed mini-split system, or full-home central air conditioning. The prices of these interventions vary widely, with window units having the lowest purchase and installation cost and central air conditioning being relatively expensive to install.

When it comes to cooling systems, remember that the expense is ongoing; home heating and cooling draw a great deal of energy. For air conditioners, that energy is in the form of electricity. You must consider monthly electricity expenditures as part of the cost of your home cooling system.

Snow Removal

If you live in an area that doesn't regularly experience freezing temperatures and snowfall, then you may want to skim over this section. However, for those home owners who do expect snow each year, preparing for its removal is a crucial annual task.

The first step is to ensure you are well stocked with ice melt or salt for walkways. You should also have a sturdy shovel designed for snow. That may be enough if you're only responsible for removing snow from a sidewalk, porch, balcony, or very small driveway. However, if you face the task of removing snow from a larger area, you may need additional preparation.

Keeping multiple shovels on hand allows you to recruit family and friends to help with snow removal. On the other hand, investing in a snow blower may be worthwhile if you anticipate frequent, heavy snowfalls that must be removed from a large area. If you have an exceptionally long driveway or other large space from which you must clear snow, you may want to consider hiring a professional snow removal service to do that job for you. Call around to get estimates and lock in your service early in the fall. If you wait until the first snowfall to solicit a snow removal service, you may find that you're too late to be added to their client roster.

It's also important to monitor snow removal on your roof as well. This becomes particularly critical when temperatures fall, and the snow hardens into ice. While icicles can create a pretty view out the window, they can wreak havoc on the integrity of your roof and gutters.

Ice that builds up at the edges of a roof can work its way into and between the elements of your roofing and gutter systems. As that ice accumulates and expands, it can break roof tiles and gutters off your home. This can create damage to your siding and lead to potentially devastating leaks through the roof.

Whenever the temperature gets very low, and especially after a snowfall, visually inspect your roof for signs of ice buildup. If it's safe for you to access those areas of the roof, then you may be able to remove the ice yourself. If you can't safely access those areas, however, then you should call in a professional to deal with any existing ice dams before they damage your home.

[25] INSTALLING AND MAINTAINING IRRIGATION SYSTEMS

Irrigation systems are typically a "want to have" feature of a home rather than a "must have." However, for some home owners it makes sense to install an irrigation system on the property. This might apply to you if you have a large garden or frequently travel. Whatever the reason for installing a home irrigation system, it will be a major financial investment and one that should, like any other investment, be undertaken wisely.

There are some simple irrigation systems that you can purchase and install yourself. Most hardware stores sell irrigation hoses that have tiny holes for water to spray out. Other irrigation hoses look like regular hoses but are made of a more porous material so that water consistently seeps out from all sides when the water is running.

Those irrigation hoses can be attached to any regular hose faucet outside your home and can be left in place. Your job would just be to turn on the water for a set period of time throughout the week to provide those garden beds with adequate hydration. If you have just one or two modest gardens that need watering, this type of DIY irritation system may suit your purpose perfectly.

However, if you're looking to water very large beds, wide-ranging landscaping, or the bulk of a lawn, you may need to seek out a professional irrigation service to install an irrigation system at your home. It's wise to get multiple quotes for installation before committing to any particular service provider.

A professionally installed irrigation system typically doesn't feature any above-ground hoses. Instead, the water runs underground through pipes and comes up through the ground at strategically chosen locations through a sprinkler system. These systems may feature several different types of sprinklers, such as long-reaching sprays for open lawns and gentle mist sprinklers for more contained flower beds. Many of these systems can then be set up to turn on and off on a predetermined schedule that you control either from a unit in your home or through an app on your phone or computer.

While a professionally installed irrigation system is unarguably convenient, bear in mind the cost of the water it will consume. Additionally, these irrigation systems require professional servicing at least twice per year: once in the fall to shut down the system before temperatures reach freezing (if applicable) and again in the spring to restart the system for the summer.

[26] PEST CONTROL FOR YOUR YARD

You may do everything right when maintaining your yard throughout the year—you diligently rake the leaves, water your gardens, and mow your lawn. Yet these efforts can be derailed by the intrusion of yard pests that leave your lawn or gardens looking messy or even diseased.

Many types of pests can invade your yard. These include insect species, rodents, and even larger mammals such as deer. Many animals find grass, clover, and other greenery to be appetizing and will happily graze your lawn. Rodents may tunnel under your grass, leaving piles of dirty and dead grass in their wake, while rabbits, groundhogs, and others may dig up your soil to create their cozy dens.

Some home owners enjoy the nearby presence of wildlife, and it can be fun in theory to watch these critters go about their day in your yard. However, these animals can also threaten your home if they dig near your foundation. For example, carpenter ants entering from outdoors can gnaw away at your home's internal structure, and the holes dug by moles and rabbits can become hazardous when they cause you to twist an ankle while walking across your lawn. For these reasons, you will want to keep a close eye on the animals inhabiting your yard.

There are several ways to deal with yard pests. These range from mechanical to chemical interventions meant to either deter or harm those pests when they enter your yard. Depending on the types of animals invading your yard and the amount of concern they cause, you will need to choose the best approach.

Fencing is a common method to discourage an animal from approaching or eating in a particular area. You may also want to put fine mesh wiring over plants you hope to protect. There are even products available that emit flashing lights or high-pitched noises known to be annoying to many animal species.

By positioning these in your yard, you may be able to repel some animals from your home without causing them any harm. Applying nontoxic treatments that are repellent to certain creatures like mosquitoes, ticks, rabbits, and deer around your yard's perimeter and on any garden beds may also be enough.

More aggressive measures against yard pests include the use of traps and toxic chemicals such as pesticides that are designed to harm approaching animals rather than simply deter them. Pesticides are widely available for purchase, and you can likely manage them on your own if you're only applying them to a small area. You can also contract with a pest-control company to provide widespread applications. Be sure to do your research when considering pesticides or the use of traps, as some can pose a danger to humans and pets as well as to the target pests.

[27] MULCHING AND FERTILIZING TIPS

Even those who enjoy fertile soil on their property will note that their plants tend to grow better when maintained with mulch and occasional fertilizers. Mulch is a product typically made of natural elements including wood chips, tree bark, leaves, and/or grass clippings. Some mulch contains manure or compost, while others are made of rubber.

The purpose of mulch is to strengthen and protect garden beds by conserving water, preventing soil erosion, maintaining a constant soil temperature, and slowing the growth of weeds. Mulch does this by acting as a physical barrier that lays over the top of your soil, often two to three inches deep.

This physical barrier also adds to the natural beauty of landscaped beds by creating a look of consistency. Mulch is available in a range of natural colors, so you can choose the one that best complements your home and landscape. Mulch should be applied each year in the spring.

Depending on how much you need, you can either purchase individual bags at a hardware store or order a bulk load to be delivered to your home. In the latter case, this usually results in a pile of mulch poured off a truck. You'll need to transport the mulch by shovel or wheelbarrow to the areas where it's needed. If you're buying a large quantity of mulch, the bulk delivery option is often less expensive.

Some types of mulch are available with fertilizers embedded within them, such as mulch that contains manure or compose. However, many home owners don't use fertilized mulch and prefer to fertilize separately. Fertilizers are essentially a nutritious food for plants. Many plants don't strictly require fertilizers, as they can meet their needs through soil nutrients, sunlight, and water. However, plants will often do best when given a nutrient boost a few times per year.

Fertilizers are available for both lawns and gardens, and it's important to apply the appropriate type depending on your plant.

For example, trees need different fertilizers than flowering plants, which need different fertilizers than grass. Many fertilizing treatments are meant to be applied at specific intervals, perhaps only in the growing season or monthly. Pay attention to labels to ensure you're feeding your plants appropriately.

Fertilizers come in different forms, and you can opt for the delivery method that best fits your needs. You can purchase small spray bottles of fertilizer or small packets of powder to be mixed with water for indoor or potted plants. You can also buy fertilizer that comes in the form of a powder or small pebbles, meant to be sprinkled onto the grass or soil over a larger area. For lawns and large beds, you may opt for a fertilizer that connects directly to your hose so that the fertilizer is distributed along with the water while you spray a large area.

[28] CREATING OUTDOOR LIVING SPACES

While the inside of the home usually gets the most attention, those who live in temperate climates may be inclined to create those same welcoming spaces outside of the home as well. Rather than serving only as the backdrop to a house, an outdoor space such as a lawn, garden, or patio can become the star of the show for relaxation and entertaining.

Since an outdoor space may not be the first place you think of when seeking a place to relax, it's important to create outdoor spaces that are inviting. While your décor decisions should fit your own personal style and preferences, some general tips will go a long way as you design your outdoor space.

First and foremost, consider your purpose for this space. Do you want a place for a group to eat comfortably outside? Are you looking primarily for a place to relax alone while drinking a morning coffee or reading a book in the peace and quiet? The specific location and design of your outdoor space will depend on how you plan to use it.

With that goal in mind, choose the right outdoor spot to suit your purpose. If you want to enjoy your morning coffee and a book outside, you may seek out a spot that is shaded and perhaps away from the main home. Alternatively, if you want to eat outdoors with your family, keep things close to the home since you'll carry food and place settings back and forth.

Even if you've chosen the perfect spot, you should prepare for unpredictable weather or climactic elements. Position a large umbrella nearby in case a day is especially warm or if there's an unexpected rain shower. Choose comfortable furniture designed specifically for outdoor use so that you can avoid rust or rot in damp weather. Also, keep in mind that a space that becomes too cluttered with unnecessary chairs or tables will be less inviting than a space that's perfectly suited to its purpose and capacity.

Lastly, think through the lighting elements that make the most sense for your space. String lights can be especially inviting in the evening, while solar path lights help to ensure that walkways remain safe and well-lit. Battery-operated lanterns or outdoor lamps can also be a good choice for many outdoor spaces.

CHAPTER FOUR: HOME SAFETY AND SECURITY

[29]
SMOKE AND CARBON MONOXIDE DETECTORS

Every home must be equipped with working smoke detectors. This is a non-negotiable, inexpensive step in home safety. As their names imply, smoke detectors exist to alert you when smoke is present in the air, possibly signaling a fire in the home.

Likewise, carbon monoxide detectors will alert you to the presence of that toxic chemical, which can emanate from gas burners, vehicles, and other common sources within the home. Not all homes have gas or an attached garage, but it's still a good idea to install a carbon monoxide detector. You never know when you might need an emergency generator or another piece of equipment you didn't anticipate having near your home.

Most smoke detectors are relatively flat, round devices that run on batteries. You install them by screwing them onto the ceiling in rooms throughout your home. The kitchen must contain a smoke detector, as must each bedroom in the home. The carbon monoxide detector may be a small unit that plugs directly into an electrical outlet in your home. These should also be placed within 10 feet of each bedroom and by any attached garage that exists on the home.

Both types of detectors will alert you to the presence of their respective safety threat by emitting a loud warning noise or alarm. Some will speak words out loud and continue to do so until you actively turn them off. Most detectors will also emit smaller noises and/or flashing lights to let you know when their batteries are running low.

It's a good idea to change the batteries in smoke detectors every six months, regardless of the battery status. Carbon monoxide detectors should be replaced every six to eight years.

[30]
TIPS FOR SECURING YOUR HOME

Depending on the type and location of your home, you may choose to invest in different kinds of security equipment to prevent break-ins. As a baseline, each door should be equipped with strong bolts, and each window should lock firmly. Some home owners also opt for alarm systems and/or security cameras to alert them to potential security issues.

There are many home security systems that you can purchase and install on your own. For example, if you want a simple camera that allows you to check the front door occasionally, then a self-installed model should work for your needs. At the other end of the spectrum, home security companies can provide extensive systems that allow a home owner to view nearly any area of their home at any time, including the outdoor property.

Sophisticated security systems also allow you to remotely control certain home features and contact authorities if you suspect a problem. If you have reason to believe that there is a serious security threat to your home, or you travel often for long durations and want to monitor your home remotely while you are away, one of these more intensive systems may be right for you.

[31]
CREATING A HOME EMERGENCY PLAN

You're likely familiar with the concept of a fire drill. During a fire drill, all the inhabitants follow a predetermined plan that allows them to escape the building in an orderly fashion and seek safety at a known location. While many people associate fire drills with school or work, the concept of a detailed plan to follow in the case of an emergency applies to the home as well.

To create an emergency plan, start by assessing your home's unique areas of risk. All homes are potentially at risk of fire, so every home emergency plan should address that contingency. In addition, consider whether your home is at particular risk from flash flooding, violent weather events, power outages, or other threats. Being realistic about the most likely threats will help you compose the most useful and relevant plan.

Home emergency plans should also include two main elements for each possible scenario: a communication plan and an escape plan. The communication aspect is fairly simple. You should know who to call and how you will contact them in the event of an emergency. Besides calling emergency services, who will you notify of the emergency or contact with updates regarding your safety? Identify the people and their phone numbers, and document these clearly in your emergency plan.

Your escape plan should take into consideration the obstacles that may exist in specific scenarios. For example, if there's a kitchen fire, your escape route must avoid going through the kitchen. For a flood scenario, don't plan to exit through the basement. Your escape plan should include the route through the house, the route to follow outside the house, and a clearly identified meeting point where you will stay and wait for help to arrive.

Once you have a clear emergency plan for your home, practice executing it. Everyone must be clear on how to follow the plan, and you must know how you will transport pets or those who cannot transport themselves in the case of an emergency. By running through your plan several times and repeating that drill twice per year, you will be much better prepared in case of an emergency.

[32]
FIRE SAFETY TIPS AND EQUIPMENT

In addition to having an emergency plan and smoke detectors, each home should be equipped with a functional fire extinguisher. This should be kept in areas where fire is most likely to occur so that it can be used when there's a small fire that you can reasonably extinguish on your own.

Some home owners also keep fire ladders in each bedroom. These are foldable ladders, often made of rope or another flexible material that allows for easy storage, that can be used to help you escape the home through a window. If your home has upstairs bedrooms, you may want to invest in fire ladders.

[33] CHILDPROOFING YOUR HOME

Whether you are expecting a child of your own or you want to be prepared for visitors with children, it's important to childproof your home. Doing so will help protect both the child and your home from accidents.

Covering electrical outlets and securing heavy objects that could fall on a child are the first things to tackle. Purchase electrical outlet covers, which are inexpensive plastic covers that go over any outlet that may be within a child's reach. They block the entrance to the outlet to protect a child from electrocution. When installing outlet covers, it's a good idea to get down on your hands and knees to see a room from a child's perspective. Travel around the walls of the entire room, covering each accessible outlet.

The other major danger for young children is a large or heavy object falling on top of them. This can include heavy objects you may have resting on a table or tall furniture that can topple on a small child. Secure all tall furniture pieces, such as armoires, dressers, and bookcases, to the wall using brackets and a drill. Even for adults, these heavy pieces of furniture can be hazardous.

In addition to securing your furniture, do a careful sweep through each room to look for any heavy or sharp objects that may be within the child's reach. Even if you think an object may be too heavy or too high for a child to access, it's better to move it elsewhere.

[34]
PROTECTING YOUR HOME DURING VACATIONS

While the prospect of a vacation can be thrilling, you might find yourself worrying about the security of your home while you're away. With a little bit of planning, you can set your mind at ease and focus all your attention on the vacation.

To start, consider whether you plan to leave your home empty or if would prefer to have it occupied while you're away. If you have pets at home that will require care, you can arrange for a house sitter to stay in your home while you're gone. This option gives you peace of mind, as you know someone will be on the lookout for any problems within the home, and they can provide you with regular updates.

Similarly, you could ask a friend, neighbor, or professional pet sitter to stop by your home once or twice per day. They could perform small tasks like bringing in the mail and watering plants while also checking to ensure that everything is secure and in order.

If you prefer to leave your home unoccupied, then be mindful of efficiency and security when leaving your home on vacation. For example, determine a moderate temperature for your thermostat. If you're traveling in the winter, you will need to keep your home warm enough to protect the pipes from freezing but not so much so that you're wasting precious resources on heating an empty home. Make sure that all windows and doors are firmly locked before you leave and activate any existing security systems so that you can monitor your home while you are away.

It's also a good idea to notify the post office that you'll be on vacation by putting your mail on hold for the duration of your trip. If you fail to do so, the mail may pile up and overflow your mailbox over the course of a few days, which can tip off potential intruders to the fact that you're not home. Use timers on some of the lights both inside and outside your home to make it look like someone is there.

[35]
UNDERSTANDING HOME INSURANCE POLICIES

While home insurance isn't required by law, most lenders require homebuyers to obtain home owners insurance on their new home for the mortgage to be approved. Even for home owners who don't have a mortgage, home insurance is still beneficial.

Home insurance exists to help you pay for damage that may occur to your home or property. These policies typically cover the home itself, as well as the items inside the home, and provide liability coverage in case anyone is injured while on your property. This can include damage to the structure of your home and/or your belongings due to violent storms, fire, earthquakes, fallen trees, and some other accidents.

Damage due to these incidents can be costly to repair, which is why having home insurance is so important. Each policy will be structured somewhat differently, so read all the fine print and make sure you understand what is and isn't covered by your policy. Like many other types of insurance, home insurance usually specifies a deductible amount on your policy. The deductible is the amount of money you must pay out of pocket before your insurance is activated to cover the rest of the expenses that accrue from a particular event.

[36]
SPECIALIZED HOME INSURANCE

Depending on the features of your home as well as its geographic location, you may need to seek out specialized insurance. There are many types of specialized home insurance in addition to the general coverage described above.

One specialized category of insurance is based on property type. This may include condo insurance, renters' insurance, mobile home insurance, or historic home insurance. If you own a condo or mobile home, investigate the types of insurance coverage that are specific to that property type. For example, historic homes may have unique construction features and maintenance costs that differ from those of newer homes.

It's also possible to purchase home insurance that is specifically for high-value homes, such as those that contain significant works of art or jewelry. Likewise, earthquake and flood insurance plans, as their names suggest, offer coverage for homes located in areas that are highly susceptible to natural disasters.

Finally, if you plan to rent out your home, then you will want to consider purchasing home-sharing insurance, which helps to cover your home against damage resulting from short-term renters.

[37]
EMERGENCY PREPAREDNESS FOR NATURAL DISASTERS

Learning about the types of natural disasters that could impact your property is an important part of the home-buying process. Natural disasters include floods, hurricanes, tornadoes, earthquakes, wildfires, droughts, and tsunamis, among others. Many of these occur in predictable locations.

For example, tsunamis only threaten property along the coasts, and some areas are far more prone to wildfires and droughts than others. If you've already lived in a particular region for a long time, you're likely familiar with the natural disasters that present the greatest risk. If you're moving to a new area, you should talk to your real estate agent as well as the locals to understand which weather events pose the greatest risk.

Once you know which natural disasters are most likely to impact your property, you can take steps to prepare. For example, you can buy a generator if the power often goes out due to hurricanes, or you can focus on clearing vegetation around your home to slow the spread of wildfires during the dry season.

[38]
KEEPING YOUR HOME WELL LIT

We may often think of lighting as a matter of ambiance and design, and a beautiful lamp or well-placed lantern can certainly enhance the beauty of an indoor or outdoor space. However, lighting is also an important element of home safety. Lighting can deter break-ins and reduce the risk of injury that results from moving around in poorly lit areas.

It goes without saying that each room in your home will require a light source. This is most often provided through artificial lighting. In some uncommon situations, you may be able to achieve sufficient lighting through very large windows or skylights. Make sure to install adequate lighting around all stairways and any other areas of the home that may present tripping hazards.

In addition to indoor lighting, the installation of effective outdoor lighting is a crucial safety feature for any home. Bright lights near all doors will help guide visitors to the entrance and prevent trips on steps and doorways. Lamp posts installed along a driveway are important safety features to avoid collisions between vehicles and other objects when the natural lighting is poor.

CHAPTER FIVE: ENERGY EFFICIENCY AND SUSTAINABILITY

[39]
TIPS FOR REDUCING ENERGY CONSUMPTION

We're all familiar with the guidance to reduce, reuse, and recycle. As that mantra implies, the first step in increasing sustainability is to reduce. In a typical home, this means reducing your electricity and fuel usage.

First, develop the habit of turning off lights and appliances whenever they're not in use. This is a simple and obvious step but one that can be difficult to implement consistently. Double-check that lights and other unnecessary fixtures or appliances are turned off when you leave a room. You can set outdoor lights on timers or use bulbs that automatically turn on and off depending on the natural light available.

The second way to reduce your energy consumption is to aim for efficiency and optimal usage of your heating and electricity when you do need them. For example, if you have a dishwasher, try not to run it until it's full. In addition to reducing the lifespan of your appliance, this inefficient usage translates to more electricity and hot water consumption.

When it comes to your heating and cooling systems, do your best to keep a comfortable indoor air temperature through smart use of your windows and window coverings rather than relying solely on HVAC systems. If the weather outside is very hot, then open the windows at dusk and leave them open until mid-morning. This will allow the outdoor air to flow in when it's cooler.

However, be sure to close the windows tightly as soon as the heat of the day begins to build. Using heavy curtains or shades to cover windows that tend to get direct sunlight during the day can also keep your home much cooler.

[40]
UNDERSTANDING AND IMPROVING HOME INSULATION

Your home's insulation is a layer of material within the walls themselves that regulates indoor air temperature. This absorbent material makes it easier to control the temperature inside your home, regardless of the outdoor temperature, by making it harder for air to move from the inside to the outside of the home.

If you feel drafts of air coming from around your windows, doors, or electrical outlets, this could be a sign that your home insulation is insufficient for your needs. Other signs that your insulation needs to be improved include some rooms feeling consistently hotter or colder than others and unexpectedly high energy bills.

Improving home insulation is typically a job for professionals. If someone comes to evaluate your insulation needs, they may start by examining your attic, if applicable. The attic is typically the site of the greatest heat loss in a home. Supplementing or replacing insulation under the attic floor can make a substantial difference in a home's overall insulation.

Improving insulation in the attic is also a straightforward process, whereas installing wall insulation in other areas of the home can be more labor-intensive. However, the inconvenience and expense are worthwhile compared to the long-term heating and cooling savings you will get in return.

Many government agencies and utility companies are available to perform home energy audits. There are also rebates and incentives available for certain types of sustainability-focused home improvements. Take some time to look into your state and local resources to find the experts and services that can help you with this process.

[41]
BENEFITS OF ENERGY-EFFICIENT APPLIANCES

The most straightforward benefit to buying and installing energy-efficient appliances is the cost savings you will enjoy over time. Energy-efficient appliances utilize less electricity or fuel, leaving you with lower utility bills every month.

Since energy-efficient appliances are generally newer models, they may have the secondary benefits of longer lifespans and improved performance. For example, newer, energy-efficient window air conditioning units are likely to be easily programmable and can be controlled by a remote or even your phone.

From a broader perspective, using energy-efficient appliances contributes to a positive environmental impact. By drawing less energy, these appliances have a smaller greenhouse gas footprint compared to their less-efficient counterparts.

If you are considering replacing some existing appliances with energy-efficient ones, be on the lookout for the Energy Star label. Energy Star is a government program that helps consumers identify which appliances are truly more energy efficient. Most appliances in a store will also provide energy ratings so that you can compare the usage rates between different brands and models. While some newer, energy-efficient models may have a higher price tag than the less-efficient options, be sure to consider the costs over the long term.

[42]
DIY PROJECTS TO INCREASE ENERGY EFFICIENCY

Below are some easy ways to increase energy efficiency and decrease your monthly bills. Many of these items we will expand on in later sections.

- Installing heavy-duty window coverings, such as blackout curtains or solid shades, on south-facing windows can be an

easy way to moderate indoor air temperature and increase the energy efficiency of your home.
- Since south-facing windows tend to receive the most light, they provide the greatest opportunity for heat to enter your home. Blocking that light can help reduce the heat that enters during the summer months. In contrast, you will want to ensure that those windows remain uncovered during the colder winter months.
- Aside from insulating your home and windows, planting vegetation can help block excess light in the summer. During the winter, when the leaves drop, it will allow more sun to reach your house.
- Insulate all pipes.
- Repairing plumbing issues will help with your water usage. Even a slight drip can add up to a lot of water over time.
- Programming your thermostat to a specific temperature will regulate the temperature in your home with minimal waste.
- Unplugging appliances after use will cut down on power consumption.
- If your water heater is over a decade old, consider investing in an insulating blanket to help it maintain the intended temperature.
- Fitting electrical outlets with foam gaskets can help prevent airflow from the walls.
- Switch to CFL or LED bulbs for lighting your home.

[43]
EXPLORING RENEWABLE ENERGY OPTIONS

In addition to DIY projects that are accessible to most home owners, there are also more intensive projects undertaken by professionals that can enhance your home's energy efficiency. For example, solar panels are appliances that are positioned outdoors in an area that gets plenty of daytime sunlight. Many home owners put them on the roof, but some models are designed to be used on the ground as well.

Solar panels capture energy from the sun during the day and provide that energy to your home. In especially sunny areas, some homes harness so much solar energy that they have more electricity than their home requires. In these cases, they can sell some of that energy back to the utility company.

Installing solar panels can be a significant upfront investment, though once the panels are installed, they often translate to reduced utility costs almost immediately. If you're considering having solar panels installed, shop around and get quotes from several companies before deciding on one. A solar company will analyze your home and the angles of your roof to determine their suitability for solar panels, and each company will have their own costs and financing options.

Wind turbines are another option for renewable home energy. Maintaining access to wind energy can reduce your reliance on fossil fuels and lower your utility costs. The upfront cost of wind turbine installation is quite high, just like solar panels. However, for both renewable energy options, there are many government incentives and rebates worth exploring.

[44]
SIMPLE WAYS TO MAKE YOUR HOME MORE ECO-FRIENDLY

There are many simple and low-cost ways to make a home eco-friendly. There is no one-size-fits-all plan for accomplishing this task; Everyone's needs and goals are different. The best way to move toward improving is by making consistent baby steps. Here is a list of some ideas to get started:

- Replace one-use items with long-term substitutes. For example, swapping out paper towels and napkins for cloth ones.
- Start recycling.
- Compost food scraps.
- Invest in reusable grocery and produce bags.
- Purchase items with minimal plastic packaging.
- Budget for replacing old appliances with energy-efficient ones when necessary.
- Re-use grey water when appropriate.
- Make your own cleaning products.

- Wash clothes in cold water and air dry them outside when the weather permits.

The path to an eco-friendly home is not going to look the same for everyone. Your lifestyle and time restraints will greatly impact which changes you decide to make. The key is to focus on building a habit of constantly improving. By changing what you can, when you can, you'll find yourself building an eco-friendly home in no time.

[45]
USING PROGRAMMABLE THERMOSTATS

Installing a programmable thermostat is another great way to enhance your home's energy efficiency. With a programmable thermostat, you can have different temperature settings for various times of day. For example, you may prefer your home to be cooler at night. The option to program the thermostat enhances energy efficiency because it allows you to set lower temperatures when you're asleep or away from home during the day.

[46]
SEALING WINDOWS AND DOORS

Another easy DIY task home owners can complete is using caulk to seal all air leaks around windows, doors, plumbing, and electrical outlets. Small cracks develop easily in those places, allowing outdoor air to enter the home. While the cracks may seem small and insignificant individually, if there are a lot of them, they can have a combined impact on the air inside your home.

In addition to caulking, you may want to install weatherstripping around windows and doors to provide a tighter seal against unwanted drafts. These are essentially strips of material that adhere to the exterior of your home, supplementing the caulk to seal off any cracks or holes.

[47]
WATER-SAVING TIPS

It's important to conserve water when trying to create an energy-efficient, sustainable home. Take short showers and encourage other members of your household to do so as well. You may even find it helpful to set a timer.

Also, make sure to routinely check all your faucets both inside and outside the house. Identifying and repairing any leaks quickly can help reduce water usage. Even if a particular faucet doesn't leak, you might accidentally leave the faucet slightly open so that water continues to trickle out. Get into the habit of checking sinks, showers, bathtubs, and hoses periodically to ensure they have been turned off completely.

Toilets are one of the greatest consumers of water in a home, and they are also prone to leaks and overconsumption of water when not functioning correctly. If you can invest in a low-flow toilet that uses less water per flush, then it's a good idea to do so. Even if you can't purchase and install a new toilet, you should check each toilet in your home regularly for leaks and listen carefully to ensure that the water in the tank isn't running in between flushes. Chapter Eight will expand on common plumbing issues and fixes.

[48]
RECYCLING AND WASTE REDUCTION AT HOME

Take part in your area's recycling and compost programs, if available. When it comes to recycling, it's important to understand exactly what your jurisdiction does and does not recycle. While it may be tempting to toss all your potential recyclables into a single bin, that may not result in effective recycling rates. Instead, take the time to find out whether you need to separate your recyclables.

If your city or town doesn't offer a composting program, you can start your own compost bin quite easily to recycle food waste into fertilizer. Buy items in bulk when it makes sense to do so and try to reduce your purchase of plastic packaging whenever possible. By investing in reusable items like multi-use coffee filters and water bottles, you can help reduce your carbon footprint in small but meaningful ways.

The best way to limit waste is to reduce the amount of material you bring into your home. For many people, this means being more intentional in their shopping to ensure they're only purchasing what they really need. By using a carefully planned grocery list, you can make sure that you only buy the food you will use during a given timeframe.

Likewise, you can reduce the amount of paper material entering your home by signing up to go digital for bills and other mail items. If you find that you're receiving mailers, coupons, or catalogs you don't want — or that can be viewed online instead — be sure to opt out of those paper mail items.

CHAPTER SIX: HOME IMPROVEMENT PROJECTS

[49]
PLANNING AND BUDGETING FOR RENOVATION

As a home owner, keep track of all the home renovations you can envision possibly wanting to undertake someday on your home. Create a list that includes both relatively small renovations like replacing a toilet and larger renovations like converting to a new heating system.

Classify each item on your list in terms of its importance or time sensitivity first. Is this something that needs to be done in the near future, or is it completely optional? Also, identify whether each item on your list is a functional renovation (i.e., needs to be done for purposes of usefulness or safety) or a purely aesthetic renovation that would simply be nice to do.

Even if your desired renovation is purely aesthetic, it doesn't mean that it has a lower value than more functionally oriented renovations. For example, you may have moved into a home with bedrooms that work fine but look dated. While this would be classified as an aesthetic renovation, having new and modernized bedrooms in your home could change how you use those rooms while also enhancing your home's market value.

Knowing which tasks are the highest priority and which are "maybe someday" will allow you to come up with a practical plan to save up for and implement those projects. Tackle the high-priority tasks first, as everything in the home must work properly.

Once you've completed your functional needs, you can save up for the lower-priority projects.

[50]
CHOOSING THE RIGHT CONTRACTORS

Choosing the right contractors for a home improvement project is an important responsibility. You are engaging these people to spend time in your home and conduct work on what is probably your single largest financial asset. You want to ensure you choose contractors you trust and feel comfortable around. They should also be able to communicate clearly and meet all agreed-upon costs and deadlines.

When considering contractors, ask your friends, family, and neighbors for recommendations. One of the most reliable ways to identify a contractor is to get a recommendation from someone you trust. You can also look online for local contractors or read some reviews from former clients. While online reviews aren't always accurate, they can give some indication of cost, timeliness, communication style, reliability, and other important factors.

Most contractors will want to meet you and view your home to get a clear sense of the project's scope and scale before moving forward. Use that meeting to discuss your expectations for the project, including the timeframe you require and a reasonable budget. While details may change as the project moves forward, you and your contractor should be on the same page when it comes to the overall vision, general timeline, and total cost.

Always get a full plan, including deadlines and estimated or exact costs, in writing before a project begins. This way, if there's ever any confusion or a dispute regarding the project details, you can refer back to the written document. If your contractor doesn't provide a detailed written contract, you can write down all the pertinent details and send it to them by email. While an email isn't a formal legal document, having such written documentation is enormously beneficial in ensuring that a project stays on track.

[51]
DIY HOME IMPROVEMENT TIPS

You don't need to be an experienced contractor to undertake home improvement projects. As long as you own your home and are abiding by all state and local requirements, including your home owners association, you're free to tinker to your heart's content. Sometimes, it's only through trial and error that you can get to a final product that you are happy with, so don't hesitate to experiment a bit.

When it comes to bigger home improvement projects, such as replacing a sink or toilet, the primary consideration is safety. This includes both your personal safety as you do the work and continue to live in the home as well as the structural safety of your house. Projects that involve removing load-bearing beams, for example, are best undertaken by professionals because of the risk of structural damage to the home.

For any DIY home improvement project, whether big or small, the first step is careful planning. Research your project carefully and talk to others who have completed similar projects before, whether in their own homes or as a professional. The more you know about what to expect from this project, the better prepared you will be to complete it successfully. Gather all relevant safety equipment, including safety goggles, gloves, and sturdy closed-toe footwear.

When you are working, remember the ever-accurate guidance to "measure twice, cut once." In other words, double check all your plans and measurements before making any change that can't be easily undone. Start with the smallest projects on your list. By starting small, you can build confidence and gain valuable skills that will serve you well when you're ready to take on large-scale projects.

[52]
COMMON MISTAKES TO AVOID IN-HOME PROJECTS

The biggest mistake home owners make when pursuing DIY home improvement projects is simply taking on too much. Starting with a complicated project as your first foray into home improvement is bound to fail. Even if you eventually complete it successfully, the experience is likely to be stressful, difficult, dangerous, and time-consuming. So again, start small, and build your confidence and skills gradually.

Another common mistake in home improvement is cutting corners. It may be tempting to skip through parts of a project that seem small, to "guesstimate" a measurement, or try to make one tool serve double duty rather than buying a separate one. All of these efforts to simplify a project are likely to backfire.

Using low-quality materials and slapdash time-saving measures can lead to problems down the road and may ultimately cost even more time and money in further repairs. Many home owners significantly underestimate the amount of time that a given home improvement project is likely to take. This can result in frustration and fatigue when a project that was expected to be quick and simple stretches on over days, weeks, or more.

However, this doesn't necessarily mean that you're doing anything wrong. Rather, an inexperienced DIYer is likely to think projects will be done faster than what's really possible. When planning a home improvement project, factor in more time than you think you will actually need. This will allow you to move through the project without feeling rushed or stressed, and you may even feel as if you were able to complete everything ahead of schedule by the end.

[53]
PERMITS AND REGULATIONS FOR HOME RENOVATIONS

While many home improvement projects don't require any permit or external approval to complete, this isn't true for all of them. Knowing whether your project requires a permit and whether it's subject to any regulations, is crucial before getting started. Permits serve to ensure that all home improvement projects abide by local building codes and meet basic standards for safety.

Home improvement projects that involve structural, electrical work, plumbing, or major changes to a home's exterior are the most likely to require a permit. Permits are typically granted through local jurisdictions such as a local building department. Check with your town or city to learn about which projects need permits and what the process is for obtaining one.

If you've hired a contractor to complete a home improvement project for you, then that person will often take on the responsibility for obtaining the permit. This should then be posted prominently throughout the duration of the project. If you're undertaking the project yourself, then the responsibility for obtaining the permit falls to you. Permits can take time to acquire and require paying specified fees. Don't forget to include these factors in your timeline and budget for the project.

[54]
INCREASING YOUR HOME'S VALUE THROUGH IMPROVEMENTS

While most home owners undertake home improvements to create a home that better suits their needs and wants for their property, these projects can also have an impact on your home's resale value. Sometimes, home owners who are planning to sell their homes within a year or two opt to take on some key home improvement projects specifically to boost the home's market value.

In addition to thinking through your own motivations for a particular project, whether functional or aesthetic, you can also think about your potential return on investment, or ROI. ROI represents the amount of increased value you can expect a project to add to your home.

Some home improvement projects are known to reliably add significant value to a home. These include garage door replacements, kitchen remodels, bathroom updates, and siding replacements. All of these provide a big bang for your buck and often have an impact on appearance as well as function.

Adding a deck to your home, finishing your basement to increase living space, and adding energy-efficient upgrades like solar panels can also be good investments in terms of market value. Finally, projects that significantly improve your home's curb appeal can have a strong ROI as well. Prospective buyers are influenced by attractive photos of a home, and a house that looks inviting when viewed from the street tends to attract higher offers than one that doesn't.

[55]
KITCHEN RENOVATION TIPS

Kitchens tend to be among the most-used spaces in a home, so it's important that the kitchen is designed and organized to suit the needs of a home's inhabitants. Perhaps for this reason, kitchen renovations are among the most common home improvement projects, and as mentioned above, can have a good ROI for those considering selling their home soon.

However, kitchen renovations can also become expensive very quickly due in part to the quality of materials involved in these projects. Since they have the potential to involve both electrical and plumbing systems, these projects are also likely to require permits and often are best undertaken by professional contractors.

When thinking through your kitchen renovation plans, the first step is to identify a realistic budget that works for you. The harder part is sticking to that budget. Costs go up quickly in kitchens, so being committed to your budget from the outset is an important part of approaching kitchen renovations responsibly.

Take time to consider what you need and want from your kitchen renovation. Do you need more space for people to gather in your kitchen or more space to store cooking equipment? Is your kitchen poorly lit or poorly ventilated and you're hoping to rectify those problems through the renovation? Sketch out your ideas for a new kitchen and continue brainstorming until you're sure the new design accomplishes your goals.

Since kitchens are so heavily used, it's a good idea to prioritize function and durability. For example, think about the placement of cabinets and which items (e.g., plates, utensils, pots, and pans) you need to have easily within arm's reach. Try to organize your kitchen to reduce the number of steps you need to take and doors you need to open to access your most commonly used items. Choose countertops that will be durable and ideally stain resistant.

[56]
BATHROOM REMODELING IDEAS

Bathrooms tend to be smaller in terms of square footage than other rooms in the home, making bathroom organization and design very important. You want to be able to easily access all items and fixtures in the bathroom, ideally without feeling too crowded within the space. Spend some time looking at pictures and floorplans for bathrooms roughly the same size as yours online. You can also speak with a professional who can sketch out some options to help you envision how your space may appear after a renovation.

If you plan to entirely remodel your bathroom, you may need to decide on a new shower or tub. Think realistically about your needs: If you enjoy relaxing in the tub or you have children or pets who need baths, then opting for a spacious bathtub likely makes sense for you. However, if a shower provides for all your usual needs, then you can save some space (and probably some money) to put toward other fixtures by opting for just a shower stall.

When choosing materials for a bathroom, it's usually a good idea to focus on materials that are durable, scratch-resistant, and easy to clean. All the major surfaces in a bathroom should be made of water-resistant materials.

Be creative when it comes to bathroom storage solutions. These can include wall storage, vanities, and under-sink storage. You may even be able to add shelving units and more depending on the space available.

[57]
DRIVEWAYS AND WALKWAYS

If your home features a driveway and/or outdoor walkways throughout the property, keeping these in good condition is an important part of home ownership. Renewing these surfaces can be a good project for an intermediate DIYer and can have a good ROI when it's time to resell the home.

Both driveways and walkways need to be routinely maintained by keeping them clean of debris and excess dirt. These areas should only be cleaned with water on clear days when they are likely to dry quickly. This is because water is the enemy of a driveway or walkway. Water can seep into small cracks within these surfaces and widen them over time, creating an eyesore and threatening the integrity of the driveway or walkway. Use a crack sealant to seal up any cracks that appear before they have time to enlarge.

Home owners in cold climates may use salt on their driveways and walkways to melt ice, and this is an effective way to reduce the risk of slipping in winter. However, salt can damage concrete and should be used sparingly, if at all, on those surfaces.

Asphalt driveways need to be fully resealed every few years, and concrete driveways can also benefit from periodic resealing. If your driveway is small, you may be able to undertake this project on your own or with the help of friends. However, most home owners have their driveways resealed by professionals due to the difficult nature of the task.

[58] IMPROVING CURB APPEAL

Curb appeal refers to the immediate impression your home gives to passersby, including prospective buyers. Curb appeal is an especially important consideration for those who want to sell their home, but many home owners want to ensure that their home makes a good impression on those passing by even if their home isn't on the market. Maintaining a tidy appearance can provide personal pride and satisfaction and also drive up overall home values in your neighborhood.

In general, positive curb appeal is made up of an appearance of cleanliness, visual coherence, and attractive colors and layouts. You don't need to have a particular eye for design to ensure that the street-facing portion of your home remains tidy. Consider removing any unnecessary items from your front porch and walkways, and make sure to perform regular maintenance on siding, driveways, and doors to prevent major structural problems.

Other projects that can help to enhance your home's curb appeal include cleaning your siding regularly or adding a fresh coat of paint to the front door. Adding a new doormat or attractive hardware to the door itself are also easy ways to create an inviting look.

Make sure that your yard and any visible landscaping remain free of weeds and ensure that all front-facing windows are kept clean and regularly caulked. If you have the option to add attractive outdoor lighting near the door and along paths, that can go a long way toward making your home appear welcoming and attractive during the day and night.

CHAPTER SEVEN: INTERIOR DESIGN AND DECORATING

[59]
BASIC PRINCIPLES OF INTERIOR DESIGN

There isn't a singular approach to interior design that works for all home owners. Design is a matter of personal preference, tastes, and priorities, so a successful design will look different from home owner to home owner. However, some basic principles serve as useful guides for all design styles.

The first of these is a sense of proportion or scale. In most cases, it's important to balance the size of the room with that of the objects placed within it. For example, a particularly small bedroom will be most functional and aesthetically pleasing if it has appropriately sized furniture rather than large pieces.

Harmony is another basic principle of interior design. This refers to the sense of visual cohesion such as having similar color tones that naturally work together throughout the home. Additionally, it's a good rule of thumb to maximize natural light wherever possible and, when using artificial light, to do so effectively for your space.

Finally, remember that your goal is a successful combination of form and function. Your spaces should have an appearance that is appealing to you and reflects your personal style, but they should also work for you and fit your everyday needs.

[60]
TIPS FOR CHOOSING PAINT COLORS AND FINISHES

Choosing a paint color for your walls may seem like a simple task. However, any home owner who has tackled interior painting knows that there's much more decision-making than you might expect at the outset. While you may have a sense of the color you would like to use in a particular space, it's important to consider the nuance of the color that you will ultimately put on your walls.

For instance, the appearance of a color is heavily influenced by the space where it appears, especially by the amount and type of lighting that hits it throughout the day. For example, if you want to choose yellow paint, then keep in mind that while it might look buttery in the morning light, it can appear greenish or white under artificial lights in the evening.

Since the appearance of colors can be difficult to predict, many stores will allow you to bring home paint samples so that you can test each color out on your walls before fully committing. Bring home a few small sample cans of paint colors you are considering and apply that paint to areas throughout the room. You should test it on different walls and see how it looks when light hits it throughout the day.

In addition to considering the nuances of paint color, you will have to select a paint finish for each color as well. This refers to the feel and appearance of the coat of paint once it dries on your wall, specifically the extent to which it has a matte or shiny finish. Matte finishes are often the least expensive and work well for living rooms, bedrooms, home offices, and ceilings.

Since a matte finish doesn't offer any shine or gloss, it can contribute to a warm and cozy feeling. In contrast, go for a higher gloss or satin finish in very high-traffic areas that are likely to be touched often. The shiny effect created when this type of finish dries can make the room seem brighter while also deflecting fingerprints and other stains.

[61]
DIY DECORATING IDEAS

Applying a simple coat of paint to any room is a terrific DIY decorating idea. It's relatively inexpensive, doesn't require a great number of specialized supplies, and is a skill that even a novice can master quickly. Some DIYers like to get creative with their painting throughout the home, such as using sponge effects to create a sense of texture. A technique like this can add personality and flair to a space without undue complexity and cost.

There are many great DIY approaches to wall décor. Some are as simple as creating a gallery wall of your personal photos. Many home owners like to use wallpaper to reflect their personal style throughout a home as well. While wallpaper can be tricky and time-consuming to apply yourself, it's possible to do so, especially if you can benefit from the guidance of someone who has experience.

There are also a wide array of contact papers and pre-glued wallpapers available to make this task easier. Some of these are easily removable, offering a home design project that can have dramatic results with little long-term commitment.

When it comes to painting, remember that the uses of paint aren't restricted to walls. You can paint floors, cabinets, ceilings, and furniture to update the appearance of any room. There are some special recommendations and techniques when painting elements like cabinets and floors, so be sure to do some research before getting started.

[62]
ARRANGING FURNITURE FOR FUNCTIONALITY AND AESTHETICS

One of the simplest ways to update a space in your home is simply to rearrange the furniture within it. This project is free, doesn't require much time, and is easily undone (or redone) if you're not satisfied with the result.

When it comes to arranging furniture, like many other elements of home style, there isn't just one correct approach. You may enjoy the visual contrast that results from pairing different shapes and textures, or you may prefer a look that is more streamlined and consistent. The most important element to consider is functionality. Items should be placed where you're going to use them or near other items you will use at the same time.

Furniture should also be spaced throughout the room in a way that doesn't impede travel. In practice, this usually means placing some type of flat surface (e.g., a side table, desk, or stand) next to any seating. However, the choice of style and type of seating and surface can be left to your personal preferences.

You will need to be able to walk conveniently through each space in your home, so consider your most-traveled routes and place furniture in relation to that route. Try to avoid blocking the path if possible.

[63]
INCORPORATING PERSONAL STYLE INTO YOUR HOME

Since everyone's style is unique, personal style shows up differently from one home to another. Some home owners enjoy shopping for décor and express their personal style through knickknacks, works of art, and textiles. Other home owners decorate with personal elements such as personal photography, children's artwork, and handicrafts.

Remember that, to some extent, personal style is expressed through every decision you make about the interior of your home. To that end, you should feel empowered to get creative and add personal touches. Naturally, your choices of floor coverings, window treatments, furniture, and artwork will reflect your style.

However, remember that your personal style is also reflected in things like houseplants positioned throughout the home, decorative drawer and cabinet pulls, the style of faucets and plumbing fixtures, and the use of throw pillows and blankets. Personal style also comes through in the items you choose to display, whether that's your library of books or your collection of baseball memorabilia.

[64] DECORATING ON A BUDGET

While reflecting on the ability of any item to convey personal style, bear in mind that it doesn't have to be expensive to decorate a home. Creatively display the items you already own or those you can make yourself to add flair without any additional cost. You can frame your own photographs, artwork made by family members, or unique leaves and other natural elements to create wall art on a budget. You can also use inexpensive houseplants, especially those that are easy to propagate, to warm up any space.

If you do want to purchase or otherwise obtain new items to decorate your home, consider finding used items that fit your tastes. Yard sales, online marketplaces, and thrift stores can be gold mines when it comes to unique home décor on a budget. Be sure to thoroughly clean any used items when bringing them into your home.

[65]
CHOOSING WINDOW TREATMENTS

Window treatments not only control the flow of light through your windows, but they're also used to decorate the interior of the windows themselves. Some of these are functional in nature, such as blinds and room-darkening curtains, while others are purely decorative.

When choosing a window treatment for a particular window, it's important to identify whether you need a treatment that serves a functional purpose or whether a purely decorative option is sufficient for your needs. Ask yourself: Do I need to block the light that comes through this window? Do I need to cover the window for privacy?

If you answered yes to either of those questions, then you will need a functional window treatment that covers the window itself. Window blinds, shades, shutters, and heavy curtains all fit this need, and your choice between these options will likely be determined by the size of the window, the cost of each option, and your personal aesthetic preferences.

However, if you answered no to those questions, then you may only need a window treatment that fits your personal style and enhances the appearance of the window itself. You may still want the look of specific treatments such as blinds, shades, or shutters to add an aesthetic element.

With any window treatments, proceed with safety in mind. Choose cordless blinds and shades if you have children or pets in the home to eliminate the risk that can result from dangling cords.

[66]
CREATING A COHESIVE COLOR SCHEME

Colors, whether used alone or in combination with others, can have an enormous impact on your perception of a space. You may be familiar with the concept of a color wheel, which illustrates each color in relation to others. This helps to show which colors naturally complement one another and which may be more likely to clash.

Colors are known to inspire certain emotions in people and can be used to create a mood or general impression in each room. For example, the color blue is known to be associated with calm and relaxation, making it a popular choice for bedrooms. Bright colors that are next to each other on the color wheel, such as red and orange, can be overwhelming when used across large spaces together. However, they can provide a nice complementary scheme when used as pops of color in an otherwise neutral design.

You may decide that you want a room's colors to be cohesive throughout. For example, you may exclusively use shades of soft gray and blue throughout a bedroom. Another popular approach is to start with a neutral palette, such as beige walls and furniture, but then accent it with splashes of bright color.

Some people also like to maintain the same general color scheme throughout their entire home as a reflection of their personal style, while others mix things up from room to room. Experiment with your décor and use of color until you find an approach that feels comfortable for you.

[67]
USING MIRRORS AND LIGHTING EFFECTIVELY

Ensuring effective lighting throughout a home is an important element of interior design. People tend to feel most at ease in well-lit spaces, especially during the daytime hours. Keep this in mind as you consider your window treatments and seek to find the balance between providing yourself with necessary privacy without blocking out more natural light than absolutely necessary.

While you can impact the amount of light that enters your home through the strategic use of window treatments, the most significant factors that determine your home's brightness are harder to change. These are the home's overall north-south orientation as well as the pre-existing placement of its windows and doors.

While it's possible to add or remove windows, doing so can be a costly undertaking that isn't always feasible. For that reason, even if you find that your home is lacking in natural light, you may need to be creative about how to maximize the light you receive.

One way to do this is through the careful placement of mirrors. Mirrors serve to reflect light, and when placed strategically in relation to windows, they can enhance the illumination in a room. Identify the windows in your home that receive the most light at certain times of day, and experiment with placing mirrors across from, or at an angle to, those windows. When you get the placement right, you may notice that the mirror can capture the light streaming in through the window and then reflect it to a different area of the room.

[68]
SEASONAL DECORATING TIPS

Decorating your home for seasonal changes and holidays can be a fun process, and it doesn't need to be overly expensive. Since these décor changes are meant to reflect the changing seasons throughout the year, it makes sense to prioritize natural items in your décor. Many home owners enjoy bringing in fresh greenery, pinecones, and ivy branches from outdoors during the winter for a festive seasonal touch. Likewise, spring and summer flowers, or displays of fall acorns and leaves, can provide small but impactful touches during the other seasons.

If you do want to purchase seasonal décor, consider prioritizing small decorative items that are relatively inexpensive and easy to swap out. For example, you can purchase standard throw-pillow inserts and then just change their pillow covers to reflect seasonal themes.

Another approach is to replace your everyday objects with seasonal ones. For example, you might swap out your plain dishes for ones decorated with autumn-themed foliage. This can be a good option for home owners who don't want to decorate by adding more items or potential clutter into their home during certain seasons.

CHAPTER EIGHT: PLUMBING AND ELECTRICAL SYSTEMS

[69]
BASIC PLUMBING REPAIRS

You should know how to address minor plumbing repairs such as simple clogs and small leaks. The first step is to shut off the water supply to the area where you will be working. There are shut-off valves underneath the kitchen and bathroom sinks as well as on the underside of the toilet.

You need to shut off this water supply before attempting any repairs to ensure that water won't be running through the pipes as you're working. Once you've shut off the water supply in an area using the relevant valve, let the faucet run for a minute or two to fully drain any water remaining in the pipes.

[70]
UNDERSTANDING YOUR HOME'S PLUMBING SYSTEM

71. Understanding Your Home's Plumbing System

Major plumbing projects should always be undertaken by a licensed professional due to the damage that can result from plumbing mistakes. Water can be extremely damaging and can even render a home unlivable through its ability to soften and weaken structural components like floors and ceilings.

It can also facilitate the growth of toxic molds. If you're ever unsure about a plumbing issue, or if you suspect that structural or mold damage may be occurring, get an expert opinion.

[71]
COMMON PLUMBING PROBLEMS AND FIXES

If your task is to repair a leaky faucet, first identify the source of the leak. With the water running, try to identify exactly where the water is leaking from along the pipe. Once you've found the source of the leak, shut off the water supply and drain the pipe.

Dry the pipe using a clean towel so that you can work on it effectively. You may find that the pipe simply needs tightening or that the leak can be resolved by applying plumbing putty. However, if the leak reappears after these measures, it may be time to replace the pipe and/or faucet, which is a job for a professional.

When it comes to clogged pipes, your first step is to clear out any standing water to avoid mold or bacterial growth. A common home remedy is to mix a cup of baking soda and one cup of vinegar together and pour it down the pipe followed by hot water 15 minutes later. This may be enough to clear the clog.

There are also store-bought cleaners that promise to break down and remove clogs. If that doesn't work, clogged pipes can often be resolved using simple tools like a plunger or a pipe snake. Put on rubber gloves to protect your hands, and then you can attempt to clear the clog by plunging the pipe. Plunge vigorously several times and flush out the pipe with warm water.

Pipe snakes are also available to purchase at most hardware stores. Each will come with its own instructions, but the general idea is that these long tools allow you to get deeper into a pipe to try to manually remove the clog.

[72]
ELECTRICAL SAFETY

Unlike most plumbing issues, electrical repairs should always be handled by a trained and licensed professional. Faulty electrical work can lead to fires. If you notice exposed or split wiring, smell something burning from any electrical area, or notice that an outlet feels hot to the touch, call a professional right away. You should also ask a professional to take a look if you consistently have problems with the flow of electricity to a particular part of your home.

As a home owner, the electrical repairs you are likely to tackle on your own are things like changing light fixtures and replacing electrical outlets. Before beginning any electrical work in your home, turn off the power for the circuit at the breaker box. Make sure you flip the breaker switch that controls the flow of electricity to the area where you will be working.

Since breaker switches are easily mistaken, especially if they are not clearly labeled, you should also use a voltage meter to test an outlet to ensure the electricity is turned off before you begin working there.

[73]
REPLACING A WALL OUTLET

The first step to any electrical work is to turn off the power for the circuit at the breaker box. Once the flow of electricity to the outlet has been stopped, you can remove the outlet wall plate. This is a simple task that requires only a screwdriver, but you must be careful while doing this to avoid touching any wires or terminals. Once the wall plate is off, you can remove the actual outlet from its box in the wall by unscrewing it.

With the outlet pulled out from the wall, you can gently remove the wires from it by loosening them from the screws they are wrapped around. Then identify your grounding wire, which will be either green or bare copper. Make sure the ground wire is not only wrapped around the grounding screw at the back of the box but also around the green screw on the new outlet you wish to install.

Attach the other wires to the new outlet: black wire to brass, white wire to silver, ground to green. You can then return the outlet to its place in the wall, screw it in securely, and reattach a faceplate on top.

[74]
INSTALLING NEW FIXTURES

The process described above for replacing an outlet isn't totally different from what you will encounter when changing a light fixture. You'll need to unscrew the current fixture and disconnect it gently from the existing wiring. Then you'll attach those wires to their current locations on the new light fixture and fasten it into place.

The key to electrical work is ensuring that wires are attached in the correct locations so that you can create a safe flow of electricity. If you ever feel unsure about how to make those connections properly, it's best to call in a professional.

75. Necessary Equipment to Safely Perform Electrical Repairs

Electrical work requires some specialized equipment such as screwdrivers with insulated handles, wire strippers, pliers, and a voltage tester. You will also likely need electrical tape and a flashlight.

In addition to those basic tools and supplies, be sure to have other items on hand to ensure your personal safety. These include safety glasses, insulated gloves, and non-conductive footwear. Keep in mind that the normal work gloves you may already own might not be sufficiently insulated. Purchase a pair that is specifically listed as insulated against electrical currents.

[75]
WHEN TO CALL A PROFESSIONAL

While the content above can serve to guide you through some very basic plumbing and electrical repairs, you will likely find that it's best to call a professional in most cases. Call a plumber when you notice a significant leak, a stubborn clog that you are not able to release from a drain, or a broken pipe. Call an electrician if you have a major power outage or any sign of water damage or overheating on a circuit. When working with plumbing and electrical systems, both of which pose significant threats to your safety and that of your home, it's best to err on the side of safety.

[76]
TIPS FOR MAINTAINING YOUR HOME'S SYSTEMS

As with every other area of your home, the key to good maintenance is regular monitoring and preventive care. Check for signs of leaks, water damage, sparks, burning smells, or any visible distress to all the portions of your plumbing and electrical systems you can easily access.

One simple preventive measure is to be sure that each drain in your home is covered by a drain cover. This will help prevent clogs by stopping hair, food particles, and other objects from being washed down the drain. In addition, it's a good idea to descale your faucets and showerhead regularly to prevent mineral buildup.

When it comes to electrical systems, one of the best preventive measures is to simply avoid overloading your outlets and electrical circuits. While it may be tempting to plug as many appliances into a single outlet as possible or use power strips to expand an outlet's capacity, doing so can overload the outlet and lead to electrical damage. If you trip a breaker, don't reset it until you've identified the cause of the trip and have taken steps to prevent it from happening again.

[77]
UNDERSTANDING YOUR WATER HEATER

Understanding your home's water heater will allow you to maintain a reliable supply of hot water. Your home will either have a water tank or a tankless system. A hot water heater with a tank stores water and provides it to your home as needed. The downside is that you'll have a finite amount of hot water. For example, if multiple people shower at the same time, the tank can be depleted.

In contrast, tankless water heaters heat water on demand. Rather than storing a ready supply of hot water, they heat the water on the way to being used. This approach offers a supply of hot water that's theoretically endless, but it can be more costly to run.

Take the time to examine your hot water heater to determine the type that's in your home. Then you can plan your hot water usage accordingly to maximize the availability of hot water while also controlling for the costs of heating.

[78]
DEALING WITH LOW WATER PRESSURE

Low water pressure in a sink or shower can be a source of frustration and discomfort. There are many factors that can contribute to this problem, and you may need professional assistance to identify the cause.

The most straightforward cause of low water pressure is an obstacle that's obstructing the flow of water. This is often due to mineral buildup in a faucet or showerhead, which can be resolved by cleaning aerators and descaling faucets. Blockages or significant corrosion in pipes can also impede water pressure, though these would likely require a professional to diagnose and resolve.

Likewise, buildup can accumulate within the water heater itself, resulting in lower water pressure. If your faucets and pipes seem to be in good working order, you may need to have the water heater examined to determine whether it's the source of the problem.

Alternatively, you may be able to improve your water pressure by adjusting the water pressure regulator. The regulator is typically located near the water main, and adjusting the regulator can moderate water pressure within the home. However, accidentally increasing the water pressure too much can cause damage to the plumbing system, so it's best to employ a professional to make these adjustments.

Low water pressure may also result from multiple fixtures being used simultaneously. Pay attention to patterns in the level of water pressure. For example, you may notice that the shower always has poor pressure while the dishwasher is running. In this case, you may need to be mindful of which pipes and appliances are drawing water at any given time and avoid trying to use too many fixtures simultaneously.

[79]
ELECTRICAL PANEL BASICS

The electrical panel, or breaker box, is the hub for your home's electrical system. You should identify the location of your electrical panel immediately upon moving into a home and make sure that it remains easily accessible. If your panel isn't already clearly labeled, you should take the time to label each breaker with the area of the home that it controls (e.g., kitchen, living room, or first bedroom). This way, you can quickly identify which area of the home is impacted if a breaker trips.

If a particular circuit is overloaded at any given time, the breaker will trip. This shuts down the flow of electricity in that area in order to prevent an electrical fire. In that case, you will notice that one or more breakers have shifted position relative to the others. Once you've identified and resolved the source of the problem, you can reset the breaker by pushing it back into alignment with the other breakers.

CHAPTER NINE: HOME OWNERSHIP FINANCIAL TIPS

[80]
UNDERSTANDING PROPERTY TAXES

Property taxes are fees due from home owners to their local governments based on the assessed value of the property they own. Property taxes are calculated annually, but many home owners make quarterly payments.

Some home owners pay these taxes directly to their local government, but they can also be combined into a mortgage bill. In either case, home owners can deduct a certain amount of their property taxes from their total income when filing taxes.

[81]
TIPS FOR BUDGETING AND SAVING AS A HOME OWNER

Budgeting as a home owner is all about priorities. Once you've decided what you want to prioritize for your home, make use of automatic transfers to a special savings account dedicated to your home. Doing so will ensure that the money will be set aside without requiring any action on your part. If you're able to let that money accumulate automatically through regular automatic transfers, it will likely grow faster than if you have to manually transfer it each month.

[82]
MANAGING HOME-RELATED EXPENSES

Some financial advisors recommend saving 1 to 2 percent of the purchase price of your home toward maintenance and repairs each year. To calculate how much you should aim to save, calculate two percent of the purchase price of your home, then divide that amount by 12.

This will give you a target amount for monthly savings. If that amount is too much, then adjust it to the highest amount that you can manage within your budget. Set a goal to increase the amount over time until you can hit the two-percent goal.

[83]
UNDERSTANDING HOME EQUITY

Most home owners buy their homes by taking out a mortgage, which they pay off at regular intervals to the lender. Each payment goes toward both the principal of the loan (the amount you borrowed) and the interest's accruing.

It takes most people many years—often up to 30—to pay off their full mortgage. However, home owners begin to benefit from the portion they have already paid off as time goes on. With regular on-time mortgage payments, you begin to build equity in your home. Equity refers to the amount of your home that you own outright. In other words, equity is the difference between the home's market value and any remaining liens (i.e., mortgage balance) on the property.

[84]
REFINANCING

It can be beneficial to have equity in your home, and it can be put to practical use in several ways. Equity represents money that you can actually use if you choose to do so. You can access a home equity line of credit (HELOC) or a home-equity loan (often referred to as a second mortgage).

This can be done to pay for major home repairs or other expenses such as going to college. Speak with your financial institution to explore rates and options for HELOCs and home-equity loans.

[85]
PLANNING FOR
FUTURE HOME EXPENSES

Home renovations often represent a major expense, and they should be undertaken with care and consideration. In addition to the expense of materials and labor, some renovations can significantly impact your daily life while they're in progress. For example, a kitchen or bathroom renovation can disrupt daily routines for weeks at a time. When planning ahead for home renovations, consider both the price and logistical impacts of the project.

However, renovations to your home can make your home more usable and better suited to your lifestyle and tastes. Given the amount of time you spend at home, it can feel worthwhile to make the investment for comfort and convenience.

[86]
IMPORTANCE OF AN EMERGENCY FUND

An emergency fund refers to an amount of money that you have set aside somewhere safe, perhaps in a savings account, that's specifically designated for an emergency. Ideally, your emergency fund should be enough to cover at least three months of your current monthly income.

The idea is that, if you were to lose your job unexpectedly, you would have a buffer of at least three months to secure a new income stream. If you have children, it's better to aim for an emergency fund with six months of income. This fund can also be used for unexpected healthcare emergencies.

[87]
TAX BENEFITS OF HOME OWNERSHIP

Home owner tax deductions refer to itemized deductions related to your home that can reduce your overall tax liability. The existence of tax deductions related directly to home ownership is a major incentive for many people to consider purchasing a home. These deductions allow you to write off specific expenses related to the ownership and upkeep of your property.

The deductions discussed here all refer to federal deductions. However, be sure to look into home owner tax deductions as part of your state filing as well. Some states have their own home owner tax deductions related to certain types of home updates or utilities. These regulations will vary from state to state, so do your research to ensure you know which deductions you may qualify for where you live.

The major types of home owner-specific tax deductions that are worth researching include the mortgage interest tax deduction, the home equity loan tax deduction, and the property tax deduction.

[88]
PAYING OFF YOUR MORTGAGE EARLY

While each mortgage specifies a period at which it will be paid off with regular monthly payments (often 30 years), home owners have the option of paying off their mortgages earlier than the allotted time. If you happen to enjoy a major one-time financial windfall, you can use it to pay off your remaining mortgage.

However, for most people, that's unlikely to happen. More often, home owners pay off their mortgages early by paying slightly more than their required mortgage payment each month. Opting to increase your monthly mortgage payment by even $100 can take a great deal of time off the total length of the mortgage. If you have extra discretionary spending money in your monthly budget, it may be a good long-term investment to dedicate that money to your mortgage payment.

[89]
OVERALL FINANCIAL HEALTH

Financial health is determined by various factors, including your total amount of savings and the amount of your income that you spend on fixed expenditures. In other words, you need to determine how your total income compares to what you spend on bills each month.

Some signs of financial health include a growing cash balance, a steady flow of income, and a reasonably steady rate of expenses. In contrast, unreliable income, significantly fluctuating expenses, and an overall decline in savings can signal poor financial health.

One way to get a sense of your overall financial health is to look at each of these indicators. Check whether your income and expenses are consistent each month. Is your total cash (or savings) balance gradually increasing? These are very simple metrics that should not be difficult to determine based on information readily available to you.

Draft a budget that tracks your predictable income and expenses. Your budget should create a pathway to meet your medium- and long-term goals. You can use a mobile app to help you create your budget or do it yourself in a spreadsheet. With a solid financial plan and budget, you will set yourself on a path toward successful saving and overall financial health.

CHAPTER TEN: HOME CLEANING AND ORGANIZATION

[90] CREATING A CLEANING SCHEDULE

First and foremost, it's important to establish a cleaning schedule for your home. There isn't one right or wrong way to approach this, and you may need to experiment to find the schedule that works for you. Remember that the best schedule is whichever one you can realistically keep up with for the long term. There's no need to be overly ambitious.

Some home owners prefer to do a thorough, full-home cleaning once per week. This full cleaning might include picking up and putting away all loose objects around the home and disinfecting surfaces. Other essential tasks include wiping down windows and cleaning the bathroom. These should all be completed on a regular basis, and they're separate from what you might do from day to day.

Depending on your schedule and the size of your home, tackling that full list of tasks all at once may be too much to take on. Even in a relatively small home or apartment, a full clean can take a few hours. If that doesn't work for you, then you may prefer to do a little bit of cleaning more frequently.

Rather than doing a full two-hour clean on Saturday mornings, you may prefer to spend 20 minutes taking care of a single task each evening (e.g., vacuuming on Monday and dusting on Tuesday). Either of these approaches can be a great way to ensure the consistent tidiness and cleanliness of your home. Try one approach or the other, and experiment until you find the schedule that works best for you.

[91]
TIPS FOR DEEP CLEANING YOUR HOME

Deep cleaning goes beyond the routine maintenance described above and involves less frequent but more intensive tasks. Examples of these tasks include cleaning carpets, cleaning the interior of the oven, emptying and cleaning the refrigerator, and cleaning various fabrics throughout the home.

These jobs can be time-consuming and physically demanding. You may need to rent specialized equipment or seek outside assistance. For example, if your home has many windows beyond the reach of a standard ladder, you may need to hire a professional to clean the window exteriors for you. All these factors can create extra expenses related to deep cleaning.

Luckily, these tasks don't need to be completed on a weekly, or even monthly, basis. Many of them, like washing curtains and emptying closets, are annual tasks. You've probably heard of "spring cleaning," which refers to the common impulse to deep clean the home during the spring.

For many people, coming out of winter and into the brighter, warmer days provides motivation to freshen up and clean the entire home. However, there is really nothing special about the spring; deep cleaning can be done at any time of year that works best for you. Similar to routine cleaning tasks, you may decide to do all your deep cleaning at once, or you may prefer to schedule these tasks throughout the year.

[92]
ORGANIZING YOUR HOME ROOM BY ROOM

A well-organized home will reduce stress and help you become more efficient. If you happen to be naturally well organized or enjoy the process of home organization, those traits will serve you well! However, home organization doesn't come naturally to many. In fact, it can feel more like a burden rather than a pleasure.

The best way to approach home organization is to invest the effort to get organized soon after moving into a home. When you do this, you can be thoughtful about how you plan to use each area and move within your space. Once that's done, the process of staying organized should be fairly straightforward.

[93]
DECLUTTERING TIPS AND TRICKS

Decluttering refers to the process of removing non-essential items from your home. This could include anything from clothing you no longer wear to books you've already read. You can also declutter by considering which sentimental items and family heirlooms should be kept and which can be donated or otherwise removed from the home. This latter category of decluttering can be extremely challenging, but there are ways to approach it that respect your values while appreciating the emotional impact of the objects in question.

Quick decluttering involves getting rid of non-essential items that have no sentimental value and simply are no longer needed. For some, this looks like donating a book to the library after reading or passing along children's toys that are no longer age-appropriate.

Another strategy is scheduled decluttering. This refers to a planned, more intentional rotation of tidying and decluttering that happens quarterly or twice per year. Many people include this as part of their deep cleaning process. For example, you may want to schedule a few times a year when you carefully go through your basement, attic, closets, and other storage areas to identify any items that you haven't used in a while.

If you see a piece of clothing that you haven't worn in over a year, it may be time to donate it. The same goes for a piece of kitchen equipment that has been long unused or an old sewing machine you can't remember how to thread. When doing this scheduled decluttering, try to approach each of your possessions with a critical eye. Ask yourself if you've used it within the past six months. Does it make you happy when you see or think about it? Can you name a time you will need it in the next six months? If the answers to those questions are no, it may be time to part with that particular item.

The third type of decluttering is staged decluttering. This approach can be useful when you feel unsure about whether to keep or get rid of a certain item. Once or twice per year, search your home for items that fall into this category and pack them all into a box or large bag. Then put that box or bag into the basement, attic, or the back of a closet—anywhere it will be out of sight for a while. Then all you have to do is wait.

If three months pass and you still haven't opened the box, then you know you can safely donate the full container and all its contents. However, if you find that your mind keeps returning to a particular item, remove that from the box while keeping everything else inside. This allows you to manage difficult items in stages: Get them out of sight, and if that goes well, then you can take the final step to actually get rid of them.

Rather than choosing one of these strategies for keeping your home free of clutter, try to incorporate each of them into your habits throughout the year.

[94]
USING PROFESSIONAL CLEANING SERVICES

If you aren't able to stay consistent with cleaning, you may consider calling in professional cleaners. Regardless of where you live, you can likely find a professional cleaning service that works in your area. This may be a large cleaning company that operates over a wide area, or it may be a local person running their own cleaning business. Ask around among your friends and neighbors or do some online research to find the cleaning service options that are available to you.

As with other household services, it's a good idea to conduct a brief interview with potential cleaning services before making a commitment to one. At a minimum, you want to know their schedule, how much they will charge, and what's included.

If you opt for a large professional cleaning company, they may be covered by insurance to protect against any accidental damage to items in your home. Smaller cleaning businesses may or may not offer the same protection, so that's something to ask about when researching your options.

Once you've found a cleaning service that fits your needs, determine the schedule at which they will visit to clean your home. Some home owners have cleanings done weekly, but biweekly cleanings are also popular. You may decide that you can do basic cleaning tasks on your own while also preferring a deep clean done by a professional monthly.

[95]
GREEN CLEANING SOLUTIONS

Those who prioritize environmental health and sustainability may find some cleaning products concerning. Many commercial cleaning products contain chemicals that can be toxic when inhaled in large amounts or high concentrations, and some home owners are understandably reluctant to use these products around their homes.

Luckily, there are many products on the market that can clean a home just as well without the use of harsh or toxic chemicals. Some of these are specialty products you can buy at the store, while others are basic household products you likely already have in your home.

If you opt to purchase green cleaning solutions that are ready made, be sure to read their directions carefully before use. While most green cleaning products are non-toxic and may even be less irritating to the skin and eyes than traditional cleaning products, they are still designed to be strong. It's important to understand how to correctly use them and if there are any necessary safety precautions to follow before using the product.

It's also a good idea to spot test any cleaner, whether green or not, before using it around your home to ensure it won't damage your fabrics or surfaces. For example, if you just purchased a green carpet cleaner, try it out in a spot that is typically hidden—such as under a chair or sofa—to ensure it doesn't discolor your carpet before applying it widely throughout the room.

[96] DIY CLEANING SOLUTIONS

If you prefer a DIY green cleaning solution, you're in luck! You can use materials like baking soda, white vinegar, dish soap, and lemon juice to create a cleaning solution that works on nonporous surfaces throughout the home. You can even add drops of your favorite essential oils, such as tea tree or lavender, to create an aromatic cleaning product that suits your preferences.

When making your own cleaning products, there are some general rules of thumb to keep in mind. Acidic products like vinegar and lemon juice are best for glass, tiles, and any nonporous location that might develop mold. You may want to use these products when you plan to clean your bathroom and kitchen surfaces.

Abrasive products like baking soda and steel wool are good for scouring surfaces that need some elbow grease to remove dirt or other buildup. Citrus, hydrogen peroxide, and white vinegar can often take place of bleach to whiten objects, remove stains, and disinfect surfaces.

When experimenting with these products to make your own green cleaners, it's a good idea to look up specific instructions to follow. This is partly because doing so will ensure you create an effective product without unnecessarily wasting your ingredients. However, it also ensures you don't inadvertently mix materials that become toxic when combined. For example, you should never mix ammonia and bleach under any circumstances. Bleach should only be mixed with water. Any time you are combining chemicals, do so in a very well-ventilated area.

[97]
STORING SEASONAL ITEMS

Depending on the climate in which you live, you may find that you have a large assortment of items that you rotate in and out of use on a seasonal basis. If your local climate features seasons with dramatically different weather patterns, then you likely have clothing, outdoor furniture, and home maintenance tools that are suited to the different seasons.

In addition, many home owners have collections of items they use at certain times of year to celebrate special holidays. Cycling these belongings in and out of use can be fun for many people. The routine of pulling out favorite holiday decorations or swapping out heavy winter clothing for the lighter fabrics of summer can be a happy ritual.

However, all these items also need to be put away when their seasons have ended. Items that will remain in storage for several months at a time, like winter boots when the weather gets warmer, need to be stored in sturdy, waterproof containers that are pest resistant. Try to avoid storing these materials in cardboard boxes or flimsy bags that can be easily damaged. Instead, opt for hard-sided, reusable containers to keep your items safe and in good condition while they're out of use.

[98] ORGANIZING YOUR GARAGE AND BASEMENT

Many home owners have a garage, basement, or attic but not necessarily more than one of those at their disposal. As you consider the storage options available in your home, think through which areas are most accessible to you and how much you could reasonably store in them. For example, while your garage may appear large, you'll want to store your vehicle in there regularly. Don't rely so much on this space, or any space, for storage to the point that it loses its primary function.

When considering the amount of space available, remember that storage is not limited to just the floor space you see in one of these rooms. Walls and even ceilings can provide valuable storage, provided they're sturdy and you take the appropriate steps to store things safely. Shelving units, peg boards, and a variety of hooks and hangers are widely available.

For example, when storing bikes, you can simply park them in a garage or basement if you have space. You could also purchase bike hooks to hang them on the walls or the ceiling. The same goes for nearly any other item you may want to store, including basic tools, lawn and garden supplies, outdoor items like kayaks and canoes, and more. Conduct a careful inventory of the items you need to organize and then visit a hardware store to review the storage options available to fit your needs.

If you're using waterproof boxes or containers, you may be able to simply stack them on the floor of your garage or basement. You may also opt to organize all your storage containers on shelving units. Either of these options works well for waterproof containers. If the containers you're using aren't entirely waterproof, don't store them on the floor. Most garages and basements are at risk of occasionally accumulating water, and it can be devastating to lose potentially valuable items due to water damage.

[99] EFFECTIVE USE OF STORAGE CONTAINERS

When thinking through home organization, pay special attention to the amount and location of storage spaces available to you. Does your home have numerous cupboards and closets throughout its rooms, or is built-in storage limited? Do you have access to a basement or attic space for storage?

If your home happens to have a great deal of built-in storage, then your primary task will be essentially deciding what goes in each space. Do your best to place items close to where you will use them. For example, designate a work or desk area and keep all office supplies nearby.

Be realistic with yourself about your habits during this process. For example, if you know that you like to jot down notes or to-do lists while drinking your morning coffee in the kitchen, then keep some paper and pens there for that purpose rather than storing them all in a home office.

If your home has limited built-in storage, you may need to buy bookcases, filing cabinets, wall shelving, and more. You can choose the items that suit both your functional needs and aesthetic preferences. Smaller boxes, under-bed storage containers, and cabinet organizers can also provide extra space and organization. Be creative when considering where and how to organize your belongings.

CHAPTER ELEVEN: PREPARING FOR THE FUTURE

[100] PLANNING FOR POTENTIAL MARKET CHANGES

As a home owner, fluctuations in the housing market can impact you positively and negatively. For example, if home prices are soaring, then the market value of your home may increase, possibly giving you access to greater equity in your home. On the other hand, when housing prices are down, you may not be able to sell at a price that will cover your current mortgage.

Specifically, you will want to keep an eye on interest rates in the housing market, especially if you bought your home when interest rates were high. If you notice that interest rates have gone down significantly since the time that you bought your home, it might be worth considering refinancing your mortgage.

Occasionally, there are dramatic changes to the housing market. You may have heard of a "housing market crash" before. This refers to a widespread decline in home values. In other words, the average appraised value of homes across the full housing market drops significantly. Even if you're not trying to sell your home, a housing market crash can impact you as a home owner. The value of your home equity may drop precipitously if your home's worth becomes less than what you still owe on your mortgage. This is referred to as being "underwater."

For home owners with adjustable-rate mortgages, interest rates may increase during a market crash, making their monthly payments even higher. Housing market crashes are often associated with economic downturns, which only makes it more stressful for home owners who are more likely to find themselves out of work.

Home owners can often wait this situation out if they don't have an immediate need to sell or refinance. The market tends to recover after a housing market crash, though this can take some time. During a significant housing market crash, the government may intervene to provide mortgage relief programs or other resources in an attempt to prevent widespread foreclosures.

The possibility of a future housing market crash isn't something you need to actively worry about as part of your daily life. However, since it's always a possibility, this is yet another incentive to avoid buying a home that's outside your realistic budget. It's also important to stay on top of your mortgage payments and pay attention to reputable news sources on a regular basis. Maintaining a general sense of the housing market in your area can help you anticipate and prepare for any changes.

[101]
PREPARING FOR RETIREMENT

Eventually, there will come a day when your home is paid off and you are ready to retire. Before that time comes, it is a good idea to consider some important aspects of aging. How much will your annual taxes cost? Who will help with cleaning and home maintenance when you're older? What happens if you or your spouse passes? How will you pay for large-ticket items such as appliance replacements? What if your health requires special renovations in the future? These questions are difficult but asking them now will help you prepare a plan for the future. One easy way to do handle this is to start a running list of maintenance costs as they arise. By documenting your costs now, you'll have enough data to pull accurate averages from later.

It is highly advised to meet with a financial advisor at some point and discuss placing your home in a trust. A living trust doesn't just protect your home, it protects all of your assets and allows your family to forgo the probate process if something happens to you. The nice part about a living trust is that you can change your mind, remove your home, and resell it whenever you want.

AFTERWARD

We hope that *101 Things Home Owners Should Know* has provided you with valuable insights and practical tools to help you manage your home with confidence. Remember, homeownership is a continuous learning process, and staying informed is key to maintaining and enhancing your property. Whether you've used these tips to fix a leaky faucet, tackle a renovation project, or simply understand the intricacies of home systems, you're now better prepared to handle whatever challenges come your way. Your home is a reflection of your care and attention, and with the knowledge you've gained, you're well on your way to creating a space that's not only functional but also truly yours.

www.ingramcontent.com/pod-product-compliance
Lightning Source LLC
Chambersburg PA
CBHW070107080526
44586CB00013B/1219